STRANGE
WEST
VIRGINIA
MONSTERS

EROCIOUS "DOGMAN"

IT CAN RIP YOUR HEAD OFF

TRANGE

MONSTERS

ESHWATER CEPHALOPODS

WEST VIRGINIA

STRANGE
WEST
VIRGINIA
MONSTERS

Michael Newton

Schiffer Publishing Ltd

4880 Lower Valley Road • Atglen, PA 19310

OTHER SCHIFFER BOOKS BY MICHAEL NEWTON

Seeking Bigfoot
ISBN: 978-0-7643-4843-3

Strange California Monsters
ISBN: 978-0-7643-3336-1

Strange Indiana Monsters
ISBN: 978-0-7643-2608-0

Strange Kentucky Monsters
ISBN: 978-0-7643-3440-5

Strange Monsters of the Pacific Northwest
ISBN: 978-0-7643-3622-5

Strange Ohio Monsters
ISBN: 978-0-7643-4397-1

Strange Pennsylvania Monsters
ISBN: 978-0-7643-3985-1

Copyright © 2015 by Michael Newton

Library of Congress Control Number: 2015934687

Bigstock Credits: © iconspro: West Virginia State Map with Community Assistance and Activates Icons Original Illustration. © hkuchera: Grey Wolf (Canis lupus) Portrait © JanossyGergely: sloth, baby sloth poses for the camera on the tree. © PlanctonVideo: Tentacles,Octopus in back light. Shot in the wild.

Designed by Matt Goodman
Type set in Minion & Futura

ISBN: 978-0-7643-4946-1
Printed in China

Published by Schiffer Publishing, Ltd.
4880 Lower Valley Road
Atglen, PA 19310
Phone: (610) 593-1777; Fax: (610) 593-2002
E-mail: Info@schifferbooks.com

For our complete selection of fine books on this and related subjects, please visit our website at www.schifferbooks.com. You may also write for a free catalog.

This book may be purchased from the publisher. Please try your bookstore first.

We are always looking for people to write books on new and related subjects. If you have an idea for a book, please contact us at proposals@schifferbooks.com.

Schiffer Publishing's titles are available at special discounts for bulk purchases for sales promotions or premiums. Special editions, including personalized covers, corporate imprints, and excerpts can be created in large quantities for special needs. For more information, contact the publisher.

DEDICATION

In memory of cryptozoologist Scott Norman
(1964-2008)

MAP OF WEST VIRGINIA'S COUNTIES

A phantom kangaroo appeared in *Charleston* during June 2005.

HANCOCK →

BROOKE →

OHIO →

MARSHALL →

PLEASANTS

WETZEL

MONONGALIA

MARION

TYLER

TAYLOR

DODD-RIDGE

HARRISON

BARBOUR

WOOD

RITCHIE

WIRT

LEWIS

UPSHUR

GILMAR

CALHOUN

JACKSON

MASON

ROANE

BRAXTON

RANDOLPH

PUTNAM

CLAY

WEBSTER

CABELL

KANAWHA

★ Charleston

NICHOLAS

POCAHONTAS

WAYNE

LINCOLN

BOONE

FAYETTE

GREEN BRIER

LOGAN

RALEIGH

MINGO

WYOMING

SUMMERS

MONROE

McDOWELL

MERCER

Credit: Bigstock

n December 2010, e-mail correspondent essica Woods posted another piranha tory online, this one from Chapmanville, n Logan County

On November 23, 1978, a deer hunter saw Bigfoot near Hile Run Road, outside St. George (Tucker County).

MORGAN

BERKELEY

JEFFERSON

— **PRESTON**

MINERAL

HAMPSHIRE

GRANT

HARDY

ENDELETON

Jack Stonestreet was fishing along Lincoln County's Upper Mud River on October 7, 2010, when an alligator paddled past him.

The diamond darter, a new species of fish discovered in West Virginia in 2008.

Pocahontas County: In the area of the nighttime sighting there has been over twenty sightings of a huge (over three hundred pound) BLACK mountain lion.

EPIGRAPH

"Have pity on them all,
for it is we who are the real monsters."
—Dr. Bernard Heuvelmans
On the Track of Unknown Animals (1958)

CONTENTS

Chapter 1

PHANTOM FELIDS

Chapter 2

IN COLD BLOOD

Chapter 3

GOING TO THE DOGS

Chapter 4

"KEEP WATCHING THE SKIES"

>> ACKNOWLEDGMENTS

Thanks to Pete Schiffer for suggesting this installment of the *Strange Monsters* series, to editor par excellence Dinah Roseberry, and to the whole Schiffer team for bringing it to life. Thanks also to Jessica Taylor, administrative secretary with the Division of Natural Resources, and to Elizabeth Fraser, in the reference department of the Kanawha County Public Library in Charleston, for unearthing an old newspaper article that featured two cryptids for the price of one.

>> INTRODUCTION

West Virginia is a war-born state. Amidst the fever of secession over slavery, forty-one northwestern counties of Virginia's Old Dominion voted to secede from the Confederacy, cleaving to the Union while denying liberation to their slaves. That shame was finally erased in 1865, by which time the new state of Kanawha had assumed its present name. Today, West Virginia ranks thirty-eighth among US states in total population, but jumps to twenty-ninth in population density, crowding 1.85 million people into 24,230 square miles, for an average of 77.1 persons per square mile statewide.[1] However, as we have seen in other installments of the *Strange Monsters* series, those statistics tell only part of the story.

West Virginia lies entirely in the Appalachian Region, and most of its terrain is mountainous. It is the country's third most heavily forested state (behind Maine and New Hampshire), with forests covering 18,899 square miles.[2] Another 145 square miles lie submerged beneath lakes and rivers. One in six West Virginians dwell within fourteen cities, occupying only 165 square miles for an average of 1,974 per square mile.[3]

The point: in West Virginia there is ample room for wildlife to conceal itself.

West Virginia is home to nearly 830 wild species, from insects to black bears. While the state's Division of Natural Resources (DNR) strives to monitor wildlife, within their limitations, other species—ranging from the merely curious to terrifying—are reported frequently throughout the Mountain State.

We call them *cryptids*, the "hidden" or "unexpected" animals whose study is dubbed cryptozoology, and they fall into four broad categories.

First, and most common, are out-of-place animals—"oops," for short—recognized as members of known species found outside their normal range.

Next come animals resembling known species, but deviating from the norm in size or other physical aspects: giants or pygmies, radical changes in color or patterns.

Third, we have reports of living animals that should be dead and gone, either extinct worldwide, or extirpated within limits of a given area.

Finally, we hear accounts of species presently unrecognized by science, either from the distant past or in the present day. Bigfoot,

Mothman, and other creatures of the Great Unknown make this the most exciting—and most controversial—category, often prone to mockery by skeptics who believe they know it all.

One such was French zoologist Georges Cuvier, still regarded as a giant in his field. In 1812, Cuvier wrote, "There is little hope of discovering new species of large quadrupeds." As for large unknown creatures at sea, he said, "I hope nobody will ever seriously look for them in nature; one could as well search for the animals of Daniel or the beast of the Apocalypse."[4]

Alas, poor Cuvier. He did not live to witness discovery of the chimpanzee, lowland gorilla, giant squid, giant panda, pygmy hippopotamus, or Grévy's zebra in the nineteenth century. New finds continue to the present day, from every corner of the Earth—and thereby hangs our tale.

Strange West Virginia Monsters is divided into nine topical chapters:

Chapter 1 covers reports of "extinct" cougars statewide, with sightings of other large cats foreign to North America.

Chapter 2 relates sightings and captures of large reptiles, either alien to West Virginia's soil, or bearing no resemblance to species classified by science.

Chapter 3 enters the realm of "devil dogs" and "dogmen," tracking creatures that conform in some respects to classic descriptions of werewolves.

Chapter 4 takes aim at flying cryptids: giant birds, birdmen, and even more peculiar airborne entities.

Chapter 5 compiles reports of West Virginia's "white things," hulking creatures known by the collective name "Sheepsquatch."

Chapter 6 plumbs lakes and rivers, in pursuit of unidentified swimming objects.

Chapter 7 turns back time, examining remains of giant humanoids unearthed in West Virginia, and seeking to discover whether any still survive.

Chapter 8 follows the spoor of hairy bipeds popularly known as Bigfoot or Sasquatch, by no means limited to misty forests of the Pacific Northwest.

Chapter 9 pushes the envelope, corralling miscellaneous unknowns who fit none of the other categories and attempting to make sense of eyewitness reports describing them.

I hope that you enjoy the quest!

CHAPTER 1

PHANTOM FELIDS

West Virginia claims two native species of the family *Felidae*. One, the bobcat (*Lynx rufus*) is rated as "uncommon" by the DNR. The larger North American cougar (*Puma concolor couguar*) is officially ranked by state and federal officials as extinct throughout the eastern United States, with the exception of a shrinking colony in southern Florida. A third species, the house cat (*Felis catus*), was imported by European invaders and thus is considered "exotic," despite its widespread presence in the Western Hemisphere.

WEST VIRGINIA'S DNR DECLARED ALL COUGARS EXTIRPATED FROM THE STATE IN 1950.

>> A FELINE LAZARUS

EUROPEAN SETTLERS FEARED and hated cougars, as a danger to themselves and to their livestock. Everywhere that white men put down roots, the cats were hunted ruthlessly, slaughter compounded by the creeping loss of their environment and hunting grounds. In West Virginia, as elsewhere, bounties were offered for each cougar slain. The last such prize was paid in 1887, for a cat gunned down on Tea Creek, in Pocahontas County.[1] By 1900, cougars were deemed to be extirpated statewide, but that judgment was challenged in January 1911.[2] According to the *Calhoun Chronicle*:

Nat Depue, of Creston, who carries the mail between that place and Grantsville, had a thrilling experience with a huge wild cat or some other animal of a like nature one day last week. He had been delayed here until late in the afternoon, waiting for the mail sacks which were on the Harry W. [a riverboat]; consequently it was dark when he crossed the Annamoriah flats, and he noticed something following him which he took to be a dog, but paid little attention to it until it darted past the horse and ran up a tree that leaned over the road. From there the cat sprang, landing on the horse's neck clawing and biting fiercely. It hung on for a considerable distance until Nattie was enabled to kick it off. The horse became frightened and ran away, but was soon checked up and the game little mail carrier got a light and went back to look for his hat and the mail sacks which he had lost. Nattie is still carrying the mail but it is a safe bet that he will always try to get across Annamoriah flats before dark.[3] Another near miss, unreported until August 2010, involved the

great-grandmother of Josh Keys, born "in Seneca" in 1901. There is no town by that name in the Mountain State, but there is an unincorporated community called Seneca Rocks (formerly known as Mouth of Seneca) in Pendleton County. One day, in her teens (c. 1914-1920), the girl was menaced by a cougar, which her older brothers killed with muzzle-loading rifles.[4]

In 1936, a staffer from the Smithsonian Institution's National Museum of Natural History confirmed cougar tracks found near Kennison Mountain in Pocahontas County's 50,000-acre Cranberry Wilderness.[5] By 1950, DNR officials listed the cougar as exterminated, but sightings continued.[6] In 1973, with passage of the federal Endangered Species Act, the US Fish and Wildlife Service listed cougars as endangered in states east of the Mississippi River. Most state agencies, meanwhile, continued to insist that all the cats were dead and gone.

Wrong again.

On March 8, 1968, Harold Parsons found five-inch-long pawprints on his wooded property in Hampshire County, noting the absence of claw marks normally left by dogs and bears. Over the next year, Parsons found several sheep mauled and devoured on his land. In spring of 1970, he once again saw "the big prints of the mountain lion, clear and definite."[7]

In early April 1976, an Elkins farmer shot and killed a cougar that had slain one of his lambs. A DNR spokesman confirmed the cat's identity, but opined that it was a stray from Virginia or Kentucky, "where there have been several reports of sightings." Its remains, allegedly, were sent to the Smithsonian for positive determination of its origin.[8] One week later, at French Creek, a 100-pound female cougar, missing part of her tail, was tranquilized and caught alive. Some reports described that cat as pregnant; others claim she was gorged on mutton.[9] Today, some reporters insist both Pocahontas County cats were pets released into the wild, but nothing seems certain. DNR officials corresponded with federal experts on that subject, but Todd Lester—founder of the Eastern Cougar Network—writes that the DNR "destroyed all paperwork on these cougars, which leaves a lot of unanswered questions."[10]

Witness "Jim W." claims "about ten" personal cougar sightings in West Virginia, spanning three decades. The first occurred in August 1976 or '77, when he was backpacking alone on the Upper Elk River, near Slaty Fork (Pocahontas County). The cat was "sitting on a rock in the river, bathing its two front legs," then fled, leaving Jim so frightened that he did likewise, abandoning his camping gear.[11]

On January 8, 1977, while driving on Hampshire County's Frog Eye Road, Ralph LaRock saw a cougar at roadside. Four months later, on May 16, David Kurtz spotted one on a coal hauling road between Pickens and Kumbrabow (Randolph County); the cat left "two large tracks about five inches long, with no toenails," according to DNR trapper Paul Hilleary. Don Barger and his wife glimpsed a cougar on July 4th, near the Point Mountain fire tower (Webster County). On August 7th, at Frost (Pocahontas County), Pearl Nelson watched "an animal with a long tail, powerful head and dark body" eating food she put out for her cat.[12] On November 18th, Frank Tighe Jr. photographed two cougar pawprints in the Cranberry Wilderness, near Lick Branch Trail.[13]

Another witness, "B. Foster," recorded his first cougar sighting in June of 1979 or '80, near Weston (Lewis County), noting that "it wasn't too long [until] others saw it." In fall of the same year, his father saw a cougar

through binoculars, watching as it stalked several deer.[14]

Third-generation coal miner Todd Lester met a cougar while hunting in southern West Virginia, in 1983. After facing ridicule from the DNR, he began a quiet campaign of private research, finally launching his Eastern Cougar Foundation in 1998.[15] Within twelve months, he had compiled a five-year list of 673 sightings from states east of the Mississippi—none of which acknowledged living cougars in the wild.[16]

Witness "Jim W." logged his second cougar sighting sometime in the mid-1980s, while scaling Elk Mountain on an all-terrain vehicle. It was another "no doubt" sighting, and again he met denials from the DNR, concluding that the agency's posture was "ludicrous."[17]

In autumn 1985, while hunting near Middle Island Creek (Doddridge County), twin brothers "Jeffrey and Matthew L." shot a buck and photographed it, then hung if from a tree while going to retrieve their pickup truck. The deer was gone when they returned, its disappearance unexplained. A few weeks later, Matthew spied an adult cougar near his home, and father "Oren L." saw two spotted cubs soon afterward. The vanished buck's tale was resolved, they think, in spring 1987, when the brothers found a cache of deer bones in a nearby cave.[18]

Witness "Christie W." was driving over Great North Mountain—straddling the border between West Virginia's Hardy County and Frederick County, Virginia—when she saw a cougar on January 24, 1994. It crossed Route 55 in four or five bounds. She estimated the brownish-gray cat's body length at four feet, minus its "very long, thick tail."[19]

In summer 1995, while working at a coal mine in Mount Storm (Grant County), Scott Goodwin saw a female cougar with two cubs, walking along a railroad line. He estimated the adult's length at seven feet "from nose to tail, and the cubs were just following her like you'd expect." Based on that observation, Goodwin logically concluded that a male adult had also been "around at some point."[20]

"B. Foster" met another cougar in autumn 1996, midway between Weston and Jane Lew, while riding with a friend. At first, he mistook the cat for "a large, light brown dog," recognizing his mistake as they drew closer.[21]

In 1996, Todd Lester found and cast large pawprints near his Wyoming County home. The casts eventually found their way to the University of California at Davis, where

extension wildlife specialist Lee Fitzhugh examined them. On September 1, 1998, Dr. Fitzhugh reported that one print "is definitely a cougar (unless, of course, it might be leopard, jaguar, etc.)."[22]

In mid-August 1997 or '98, shortly before school convened, young "Joe S." heard screeching near his home, "like a woman and a baby just raising hell." His father recognized the sounds from bygone years, attributing them to a cougar.[23]

In June 1998, Professor George Rossback

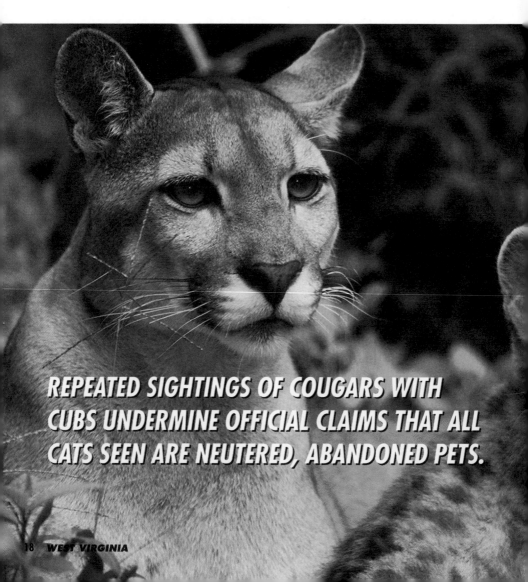

REPEATED SIGHTINGS OF COUGARS WITH CUBS UNDERMINE OFFICIAL CLAIMS THAT ALL CATS SEEN ARE NEUTERED, ABANDONED PETS.

Sr., from West Virginia Wesleyan College, found and followed cougar tracks in a wilderness area of the 921,000-acre Monongahela National Forest. Rossback did not see the cat, but his photos of its pawprints confirm an adult cougar in the area.[24]

Another case from 1998 involves witness Alice Hanna. While driving with a friend near Frankford (Greenbrier County), Hanna saw a rabbit dart across the road, closely followed by a cougar that was "beige, had a long tail, and cub like ears." She waited a decade to report the sighting, saying, "I didn't tell anyone because I knew I would be called a liar. But I know what I saw!"[25]

Witness H. C. Willis vaguely describes a cougar sighting from the late 1990s, along US Route 19 near Hico (Fayette County), but his report offers no details.[26] Josh Keys saw a pair of cougars while golfing in Burlington (Mineral County), in June 1999 or 2000, watching them for fifteen minutes as they slowly traversed a ridgeline.[27]

Tom Hahn had a startling cougar encounter, one afternoon in September 1999, while driving on the Blue Ridge Parkway near Bedford County's Peaks of Otter. The cat leaped from a roadside boulder, landing in front of Hahn's car and halting his progress for roughly two minutes. "It was beautiful," Hahn wrote. "Its long tail was dancing in the air, it was walking back and forth across the road, and it seemed to be anxious to leave, but still looking hard up the mountain." Finally, the cat shrieked at Hahn and his passenger, then scaled a stony cliff before it disappeared into the woods.[28]

April Dailey of Berkeley Springs supplies another case from 1999. While on her way to work one morning, traveling along Route 522 in Morgan County, she saw what she believed to be a road-killed deer lying beside the highway. Drawing closer, she saw that the beast was "a VERY large, light-brown-colored cat. It was probably as long as I am tall and it had a very long, very thick tail." Coworkers laughed at her description of the cougar, and its body was no longer at the scene when she drove home from work.[29]

Perennial witness "Jim W." claimed two more sightings in October 1999, followed by another pair in October 2000. A neighbor also saw one of the cats in his backyard. The sightings all occurred in Pocahontas County, two from fifty feet. Wife Betty saw one of the cougars, described as "a sub-adult" with "a winter darkish coat."[30]

Credit: US Fish & Wildlife Service

Between Jim's latest sightings, in August 2000, professional photographer "Jeff T." saw a cougar while picking berries near Moorefield (Hardy County). A deer in flight alerted him before he saw the cat in hot pursuit, running "faster than any racehorse I've ever seen." The cougar "was almost on its tail and gaining ground, a fluid streak of muscle, long tail straight behind the body...Before I could put down the berry bucket and focus my camera, they had disappeared into the woods on the other side of the field."[31]

Air Force Master Sergeant Ben Walker dates his first cougar sighting from 1999 or 2000, omitting a specific month. While traveling from North Carolina to Fairmont (Marion County) on US Route 19, at 2 a.m., he pinned a "most beautiful and chilling creature" in his headlights. "The cat was tan," he wrote, "with black ear tips and a dark tipped tail. The tail seemed to be four or five feet long, and as big around as my arm." Startled, the cougar jumped over a guardrail and vanished.[32]

"Joe S." was riding an ATV near Alexander (Upshur County), when he saw a large cat jump away from a deer carcass with its throat gashed and hindquarters partially devoured. He glimpsed the cat again, crossing a nearby field, and was "quite sure that it was not a house cat that took down the deer."[33]

Witness "Jeff" was stalking deer with his adult son during bow hunting season (late September through December) of 2000, when the younger hunter met a creature that left him trembling. He described it as "bigger than Riley (our 110-pound black lab)," with its tail dragging the ground. Jeff later "tried to talk to the DNR about it, but they said we were making it up."[34]

In October 2001, Eastern Puma Research Network leaders John and Linda Lutz reported 330 West Virginia cougar sightings from July 1, 1993, through December 31, 2000. Forty-two of those reports included cubs, a problem

for skeptics who insist that all cougars seen in the East must be pets released by irresponsible owners. "Pet" cougars are normally neutered, thus ruling out reproduction. West Virginia ranked fourth among eastern states surveyed, in the number of sightings reported.[35]

Sometime in 2002, witness Markel Fertig was driving over Kinnison Mountain at 4 a.m., when he saw what he took for a deer in the roadway. Closer inspection revealed that the beast was a large, long-tailed cat.[36] In autumn of that year, an anonymous Whitehall couple saw a cat "bigger than a golden retriever" skirt their rural property.[37] In August 2009, "Tom H." reported that his daughter had seen a cougar "six or seven years ago," while driving through Lincoln County on Route 34, near Harvey Creek. It was crawling under a horse pasture fence, its long tail clearly visible.[38]

Barbara Chaplin organized another research group, Cougar Quest Virginia, in February 2005, "to prove the existence of the cougar... in this part of Virginia/West Virginia as an adjunct to the work of various other wildlife/ environmental organizations that are researching the 're-existence' of cougars in the East." Pledged to protect surviving wild cougars without supporting reintroduction campaigns, Cougar Quest denied affiliation with competing groups, compiling data from a network of independent observers spanning both states. Sightings posted on the group's website are current through March 2014.[39]

Rumors of cougar survival in Grant County's Smoke Hole Wilderness Area span a century, confirmed by discovery of pawprints in 2005, but the DNR persists in denial.[40] In early spring of that year, witness "Luke D." and his parents found similar tracks in fresh snow, near a mountain resort's ski lift.[41]

Jeff Conrad and a friend were scouting for deer one night in 2005—"NOT SPOTLIGHTING!!!" he insists; "JUST LOOKING!!"—and had found several when their lights illuminated "a big cat with a long, thick tail that hung down low." Conrad wrote, "The complete confidence of the cat's stare and gait sent chills through my body...To this day I get the chills walking outside at night in that area."[42]

Melanie Dodson found large pawprints near her new home south of Berkeley Springs, the day she moved in during March 2005. Four months later, with her husband, she saw a cougar drop fifteen feet from a nearby tree and run into the woods. "That same summer," she writes, "I heard a deer being taken down at night in my side yard. The next morning there was a lot of blood on the ground but no remains."[43]

On June 25, 2005, Martinsburg resident "Charlow" filed a report with Cougar Quest online. Her cat had vanished two weeks earlier, followed by "an infant or cat meowing sounds" the next week, then "an actual cougar snarl" behind her home as she returned from work at 4:40 a.m.[44] Despite their size, cougars are not "big cats" in scientific terms—that is, members of the genus *Panthera*, which includes jaguars, leopards, lions, and tigers. Lacking the ossified hyoid bone common to *Panthera* species, cougars cannot roar, although they snarl convincingly and may emit unearthly shrieks when agitated.

Wildlife experts confirmed more cougar tracks from the Mountain State—this time, an adult and cub together, found near the Mount Storm Power Plant—in February 2006.[45] In late summer that year, Debbie Bond and friend "Larry" saw a cougar across the road from Bond's house, slinking after a girl and her dog. "I seen it was a cat," Bond writes, "and scream[ed] for the girl to get her dog in the house. She thought I had lost my mind but thank heavens she did what I screamed for her to do and ran to the house." The cougar then turned toward Bond's driveway, prompting her to rush indoors as well.[46]

That autumn, while searching for his cat one night in Boone County, Zachary Harris found his pet cowering and saw a "large-bodied animal" with a long tail, watching from a hillside above his rural home. It growled, then turned away. Internet research convinced him the beast was a cougar.[47]

Another report from 2006, otherwise undated, comes from witness David Walker. While visiting his grandmother in Brown's Creek Hollow, near Welch (McDowell County), Walker saw an "absolutely beautiful" cougar watching him from twenty-five yards. Walker reported the sighting to his grandmother, whereupon she replied, "Oh, you saw 'Tom'? He comes around every once in a while, but what's really scary is when you hear him scream at night."[48]

On November 8, 2006, while driving ATVs on the Pinnacle Creek Trail System near Pineville (Wyoming County), Ken Vandevort and his wife surprised a cat that stood some thirty inches tall at the shoulder, with a body more than four feet long. For those who doubt his clarity of eye, Vandevort writes, "I can assure you that what I saw was in fact a mountain lion."[49]

Three weeks later, at 7:30 a.m. on November 21, Nedra Platt glanced up from washing dishes to behold a cougar walking through a neighbor's field. It was tan-gray, its body about four feet long, with a tail to match. Platt summoned her husband, and both watched the cougar until it vanished.[50]

The year's last sighting, on December 26, was logged by hunter Chris Sparkman, six miles from Paw Paw (Morgan County). Stalking deer along a logging road, he met a cat that "approximated a yellow lab" in size and color. Sparkman's verdict: "It was clearly a mountain lion."[51]

At four o'clock one afternoon, in late spring of 2007, Eric Short and a friend were driving on Barnum Road, below the Jennings Randolph Dam (Mineral County), when they saw a cougar cross the pavement. It paused atop a ten-foot roadside bank to watch them pass, at which time Short remarked on its "somewhat emaciated" profile.[52]

That summer, date unknown, Dave Marshall was fishing with two friends on Shavers Fork of the Cheat River (Randolph County), when they spied a large cat forty yards distant. Marshall first thought it must be a bobcat, then noted its long tail and reddish color. The fishermen decided it must be a young cougar, weighing fifty to sixty pounds.[53]

John Lutz reported a find of confirmed cougar pawprints in late August 2007, along Roaring Creek, north of Onego (Pendleton County).[54] Soon afterward, in early September, retired schoolteacher Charles Keaton saw a cougar cross Highland Scenic Highway in the Monongahela National Forest, passing within twenty yards of his car.[55] That same month, while bicycling along the Chesapeake and Ohio Canal at 8:15 a.m., Rob Watt emerged from the Paw Paw Tunnel to see a cougar crossing the trail ahead. "He was trotting," Watt wrote, "and I could easily identify his large size, color, long tail, stockiness and head and the graceful movement."[56]

Two other sightings from 2007 offer no dates or specific locations. Mark Mcvicker was driving home from work at 3 p.m., when a cougar "crossed the road, jumped the creek and looped across a hay field to the woods." He estimated that the cat was six feet long and weighed more than 100 pounds.[57] Elsewhere, after Melanie Dodson's husband helped a neighbor cull nine deer from a domestic herd, they heaped bloody leftovers in the backyard. Later that night, Melanie turned on the porch light and saw a cougar thirty feet from her home, "taking full advantage of the free meal." Next morning, she called the DNR, where an officer "basically laughed and said I must have saw something else."[58]

On January 25, 2008, Krissi Wood's family saw a cougar lying in snow near the Snowshoe

Mountain Ski Resort.[59] One month later to the day, e-mail correspondent "Pat" claimed a cougar had been struck by a car on Route 14, between Grantsville and Parkersburg, then euthanized by DNR officers. Alas, the story was a hoax, including photos of an Arizona cougar killed in 1999. By March 2008, the tale had morphed repeatedly, claiming the long-dead cat had lately been run down in Arkansas, Kentucky, and Pennsylvania.[60]

In late April 2008, Brandi Heflin's mother and grandfather were driving her daughter to baseball practice in Four States (Marion County), when a cougar crossed the road slowly, climbed an embankment, then reclined on a log, watching the car pass by. On May 26, while taking out her trash, Brandi heard sounds "like a cat growling" and summoned her husband, but they saw nothing.[61]

Two days later, at 8:30 a.m. on May 28, Berkeley Springs resident "Judy S." looked out her kitchen window and beheld "what I believe to be a mountain lion/panther" walking through sparse woods toward an abandoned house, 200 yards away. The cat was brownish-gray, its body three to four feet long, with a tail of comparable length. Years spent in Kenya as a member of the US Foreign Service made her confident the animal was not an oversized house cat.[62]

In June 2008, Lowell McDonald camped near Eagle Rock, on the South Branch Potomac River in Smoke Hole Canyon. During a thunderstorm that night, he saw "a very large animal" run through his campsite. "It was very similar in color to the brown of a whitetail deer," McDonald wrote, "but it had a large long tail, all brown. It seemed to be about the size of a large dog."[63]

August 2008 favored witness Dave Marshall with a second cougar sighting. Driving through Ohio County on Harvey Road, he saw a long-tailed cat weighing 100 to 125 pounds in a roadside field. Soon afterward, a mauled deer carcass was found in Wheeling, near Cabela's, the self-proclaimed "world's foremost outfitter."[64]

On October 3, 2008, Dorothy Lane saw two adult cougars near her home on Spruce Flat Road, in Buckeye (Pocahontas County). They were "close enough to see with the naked eye, but I still grabbed my binoculars to get a great look at them."[65] On October 28, Putnam County teacher Patricia Wolford reported a cougar sighting by one of her students, living on Redhouse Hill.[66]

At 1:30 a.m. on November 12, handyman "Trevor" left his cabin at the Abram's Creek Lodge and Campground to use the restroom, but was intercepted by "a beige colored mountain lion...complete with a huge bushy tail." Man and cat stared at each other for several seconds, until the cougar bolted into darkness.[67]

Childhood ear-witness "Joe S." saw a cougar in the flesh a decade after his first encounter, during the winter of 2008-09. The cat crossed a road in front of his car, swishing its three-foot-long tail and leaving pawprints in the snow.[68] On December 26, 2008, residents of Churchville (Lewis County) blamed "at least two mountain lions" for the daylight slaughter of a horse, whose body bore deep claw and bite wounds.[69]

A final case from 2008, otherwise undated, involves a sighting by Terry and Marsha Moore near Cacapon Mountain, straddling the border of Hampshire and Morgan Counties. They saw the cat "literally leaping" across Route 522, describing it as "extremely large

BOBCATS BEAR LITTLE, IF ANY, RESEMBLANCE TO COUGARS, FROM THEIR TUFTED EARS TO SHORT TAILS.

Credit: US Fish & Wildlife Service

with a long tail, probably four to five feet at least. This was not even close to a bobcat."[70]

On February 28, 2009, Cougar Quest received a report from "Gary W.," identified as a "retired Federal Police Officer [and] seasonal employee" of the National Park Service. Gary's e-mail vaguely described a cougar sighting somewhere along the 320-mile New River, but provided no date or further details. He wrote that the "DNR and the National Park Service denied the sighting, but I was adamant!" He also recalled (but could not produce) a supposed article from the *Washington Post*, describing release of cougars in the region by the US Department of the Interior, sometime in the late 1960s or early '70s. The government denies any such efforts, then or later.[71]

At 4:30 a.m. on April 9, 2009, security guard Dana Redman spied two deer in a field while patrolling Hawks Nest State Park (Fayette County). Turning his spotlight toward them, Redman saw a cougar sitting on a nearby wall, watching the deer. It fled the light, but his sighting prompted Redman to recall a tourist's report of seeing a cougar on April 7, near the park's clifftop overlook on US Route 60.[72]

On May 23, Peter Gollihue of Huntington posted a video clip on YouTube, purporting to show a cougar at some unspecified West Virginia location. Ninety seconds of the three-minute video focus erratically on a cat sitting in forest terrain, then walking out of sight. The female photographer repeatedly calls it "huge," but the clip includes nothing to provide a sense of scale.[73]

Ian Thornton also met a large cat around midnight on May 23, while driving on Merritts Creek Road in Huntington. Thornton admits that he "did not get a great look at the animal," but says "it was much too large to be any dog and not tall enough to be a deer. Its movements strongly resembled that of a cat." Overall, he was "95 percent" convinced that he had seen a cougar.[74]

Two weeks later, on June 6, "Kimberly W." reported a sighting to Cougar Quest. Husband Donnie was driving slowly through private property owned by his hunting club on the Capon River, when he saw a cougar sunning on some rocks near Capon Bridge (Hampshire County). Donnie watched the cat through binoculars for roughly five minutes, before it noticed him and fled. He judged its length at six feet, "with a long thick tail with dark fur at the end." Hearing Donnie's report, another member of the hunting club recalled seeing two cubs near the same site, in 2007 or 2008.[75]

Kayaker "Steve" and an unnamed friend claimed a sighting from McElroy Creek (Tyler County), sometime in spring 2009. While paddling downstream, they heard "all kinds of commotion" above them and saw an "enormous" cat climbing a pine tree. Seconds later, three cubs with "really long tails and obviously a bigger build than a house cat" scurried after their mother. DNR agents insisted that Steve had seen a bobcat or a fisher (*Martes pennanti*), a mustelid that may reach four feet in length.[76]

Counselor and journalist Kimberly Short-Wolfe purchased a farm near Elkins (Randolph County) in June 2009, and logged her first cougar sighting before that month ended. With her children, over time, she identified a female adult, whom Short-Wolfe called "Lily," and two cubs, dubbed "Freaky" and "Freddie." The cats were seen "on numerous occasions by numerous individuals (some with 'expert' credentials)," and documented in a local newspaper, *The Inter-Mountain,* that publishes Short-Wolfe's columns. Short-Wolfe's daughter collected feces, delivered to a local DNR biologist, who said, "It looks just like our mountain lion scat." Short-Wolfe also snapped photos, still unpublished, which she deems insufficient as proof of lions dwelling on her property.[77]

Around the same time Short-Wolfe first went public with her story, in mid-August 2009, repeat witness "Jim W." reported another cougar sighting, from Monterville (Randolph County). A vague account of that report, published online by Cougar Quest, suggests a series of encounters between August 17th and September 5th, but the website provides no details.[78]

The third week of August 2009 produced multiple cougar sightings along the Greenbrier River Trail, winding for seventy-eight miles through Pocahontas and Greenbrier Counties. Two of the witnesses were students from Lewisburg's West Virginia School of Osteopathic Medicine.[79] On August 28th, while riding ATVs along Indian Creek at Racine, Jarold Leffel and a friend treed an apparent cougar cub. While they were watching it, a larger cat appeared. Its coat was "pretty dark," and Leffel judged its tail to be three feet long or more. At that point, he writes, "We both left pretty quick."[80]

On May 7, 2010, the Denver-based website Examiner.com reported multiple cougar sightings around Clendenin (Kanawha County).[81] Eleven days later, Wayne County witness "Tom C." claimed two sightings. His first encounter, near Buffalo Creek in March, was preceded by sounds of "something killing something up on the hill behind my house." The second occurred near Walkers Branch Bridge.[82]

On July 16, 2010, Wood County resident Jill Carden reported that a neighbor had recently seen and photographed a cat the size of a German Shepherd that "looks like a mountain lion." It was grayish-tan, with a long tail, and multiple witnesses pegged its weight around ninety pounds.[83] Later that summer, while walking his dog on a woodland trail in Randolph County, Rich Miller met "a large animal, yellow-brown in color with a long uniformly thick tail. The ears were relatively short but erect. The animal moved from a crouching position in a drawn-out 'cat stretch' and in one bound covered about twenty feet or more down the mountain side to disappear into the underbrush."[84]

On October 15, 2010, witness "Chopper Dave" reported a cougar sighting from US Route 19, somewhere in central West Virginia. First alerted to local wildlife by "a pure white ram or some type of goat" at roadside, he next saw "a mountain lion or cougar or something like that" cross the highway 100 yards farther south. Dave writes, "I am a former hunter turned animal lover so I am sure I know what I saw."[85]

On November 8, 2010, Brittany Harney-Moore reported a series of October events involving her aunt and uncle at Lahmansville (Grant County). First, the uncle heard "loud cat screams," but he "brushed it off" until his wife saw a cougar in the flesh, a week later. The cat was "thick and stocky," at least seven feet long, tail included. Soon afterward, Brittany's brother left a deer carcass as bait and caught the cat's blurred image with a trail camera. She promised "big news" after Thanksgiving, when her clan gathered to hunt down the cougar, but no follow-ups have been posted.[86]

On the same day Harney-Moore filed her report, James McCune and his girlfriend saw "a beautiful and powerful-looking" cougar on US Route 50, six miles east of Grafton (Taylor County). It sprang from a roadside embankment onto the highway, stared at their car, then turned and scaled the slope again "with one powerful leap."[87]

Two days before Christmas 2010, driving toward Oak Hill on the West Virginia Turnpike, motorist "James W." saw a cougar near the exit for Paint Creek Road.[88] Nine days later, on the night of January 1, Lacey Kingston saw another on Interstate 64, near Exit 8 to Huntington. This cat lay sprawled on the pavement, apparently dead or unconscious. It "looked like a lion, its body was long, at least four to five feet, it had a really long tail, small head, [and] it was tan in color." Kingston phoned local police, who said they would contact state troopers—and the rest is silence.[89]

Despite an escalating number of reports, US Fish and Wildlife formally announced the eastern cougar's extinction on March 2, 2011. Martin Miller, Northeast Region Chief of Endangered Species, told reporters, "We recognize that many people have seen cougars in the wild within the historical range of the eastern cougar. However, we believe those cougars are not the eastern cougar subspecies. We found no information to support the existence of the eastern cougar."[90] No longer protected, except in Florida, cougars are presumably fair game for hunters east of the Mississippi.[91]

A month after the federal announcement, on April 9, Hampshire County farmer Charlene Pietra saw a cougar on her property at Levels. She called the DNR that afternoon, and an operator told her "the managers will be in later and would call me back." So far, no one has.[92]

At 10 p.m. on May 25, 2011, Elizabeth Vansickle and her husband heard what they "sincerely believe to be a mountain lion" snarling in the shadows near their home in Leon (Mason County). Elizabeth writes that her husband "will not let me call DNR because he says they will not admit mountain lions exist in West Virginia or that they are actually reintroducing them in our state"—a suspicion shared by many residents, despite repeated denials.[93]

June of 2011 brought a sighting report from Saundra Thomas, in Mineral County. While sitting on her porch, at 12:43 a.m. on June 27, she saw an animal "the color of a deer but way too low to the ground" crossing the edge of her lighted yard. The fawn-sized cat had "a long tail almost to the ground."[94]

In early July, while driving home from North Carolina to Tate Creek (Braxton County), Linda Young saw a cougar crossing the highway at 10 p.m. Despite her husband's skepticism, she wrote, "There was no mistaking to me what it was because I was so close to it and it was moving slowly."[95]

During the weekend of July 27-28, 2011, Janie Stopford took her three dogs hiking in the woods along Three Churches Hollow Road, twenty-two miles northeast of Romney (Hampshire County). Along the way, she met "the LARGEST cat I have ever seen (except in the zoo). It was draped over a log...so that I could clearly see its face, front legs, and forward body. It was larger than my Belgian Sheppard, uniformly tan, had a round face (which looked too small for its body), round, small ears, and white on the front paws." She slowly retreated when the cat began eyeing her dogs.[96]

On August 1, 2011, while driving east on Route 66 near Cass (Pocahontas County), Jerome Kay and his nephew saw a dark gray cougar, four or five feet long including its tail, cross the highway and vanish into the forest.[97]

Three months later, on November 6, Lori Andrews and her husband visited their newly purchased property at Great Cacapon (Morgan County), and were greeted by a handmade sign on Rock Ford Road that cautioned: "Be alert there is a mountain lion in here! I saw it! Beware!" They called the former owner, who admitted seeing two cats in October.[98]

Six days later, Roger and Crystal Hamrick were geocaching in Harrison County's Laurel Park. The game involves a treasure hunt of sorts, using GPS coordinates to find log books cached at various locations, signing them, and leaving them in place. On Presley Ridge, a panicked deer distracted them, followed immediately by a leaping cougar. They described the cat as being "a dark yellow, goldish color," larger than their Australian Shepherd. "The tail seemed to be longer than its body and curving down and back up again."[99]

At 1 a.m. on December 4, 2011, while wrapping up a raccoon hunt, Bryan Burkhamer and a companion saw a large cat near their pickup truck. "It stood about three to four feet tall [with] a long tail," Burkhamer wrote. "It was tan, black tipped tail. It circled our truck then it kept walking up the road. Definitely not a bobcat."[100]

Diane Asmus reported a cougar sighting from Huntington on February 15, 2012. She saw the cat in a wooded valley near Seneca Ridge Townhomes, on Mohawk Court, where she lived with her in-laws. The cat was "huge," sporting "a really long tail" with white hair at its tip.[101] Eight days later, Mark Christian and his girlfriend met a cougar while driving on Corridor G, seven miles outside Chapmanville. The "mountain lion of considerable size" startled Christian so badly that he swerved and nearly crashed his car.[102]

Kimberly Rice met her cougar at 11:45 p.m. on March 27, 2012, on Bingamon Road in Marion County. It climbed a tree while still illuminated by her headlights, revealing a tan coat and "a black tipped long tail that dipped slightly after it left the hindquarters. I had too good of a look for anyone to say it was anything else."[103]

Four days later, Lisa Brooks Fausey saw a cougar prowling behind her Berkley County home, a mile outside Martinsburg. Her dachshund chased the cat, returning with a deep gash on its rump that required twelve staples to close.[104]

On April 17, 2012, Greenbrier County artist Mark Cline belatedly reported a childhood sighting from Simms Mountain Road in Rainelle. The cat was large, "blond in color and its tail was about four feet long." The memory came back when Cline's daughter proposed writing a class report on West Virginia cougars and "the teacher would not accept it. He said if anyone tried to present him with evidence he would call them a liar."[105]

At 12:30 a.m. on June 5, 2012, after fishing at Springfield's Hanging Rock (Hampshire County), Jeff Paugh and two cousins met a cougar near their car. Paugh's description of the cat (unedited) describes "a mountain lion, tannish color with white belly about six to seven feet length an what we guesstimated at least 100 pound long tail black tip. I know the experts say they don't exist around these parts but we know what we seen and it wasn't a bobcat I've seen plenty of them to know what a bobcat looks like and was definitely not a dog."[106]

Three weeks later, on June 25th, Suzanne Jones reported a cougar at large outside Charleston. She glimpsed "the rear end with long tail of a very large cat" and called police, who referred her to the DNR, but as in Charlene Pietra's case, that agency ignored her call. Neighbors told Jones they had seen an adult cougar with a cub on several occasions.[107]

On September 1, 2012, Cheney Allman reported a cougar sighting from Fernow Experimental Forest near Parsons (Tucker County). Her boyfriend was driving when Allman saw the cat scaling McGowan Mountain. "We had several clear unobstructed views of it," she wrote, "and I have to say it was beautiful."[108]

Anne Shearin was driving near Gerrardstown (Berkeley County) when she saw a long-tailed, "golden yellow" cat cross the road on March 10, 2013.[109] Cora Moose caught a cougar on film, with a trail camera, on June 9th, but neglected to say where the photo was snapped.[110] Connie Russell was "back road touring" near Clover Lick (Pocahontas County) on September 11th, when a "gorgeous" long-tailed cougar crossed her path.[111]

A month later, on October 15th, news broke of a cougar mauling domestic animals around Falling Waters. Victims in the spree included two miniature horses and a donkey. DNR spokesmen and Berkeley County Animal Control blamed the attacks on "wild dogs," but local witnesses demurred. Caitlyn Harmison saw the cougar in her backyard, getting "a really good shot of its back and its tail," preserving pawprints that measured four by five inches. Another witness, Aaron Whittington, said, "I've never seen a dog crouch down and the back was arched, the tail was sticking straight up and its neck I'd say two feet long neck and its body length was at least me [*sic*]. It was a 150-pound cat."[112] Sheriff Kenneth Lemaster Jr. told reporters, "We've got people who are pretty positive that they've spotted a mountain lion or a cougar, but, you know, its kind of hard for us to confirm something like that when we don't have a picture or we don't have anything specific."[113] Traps set for the cat remained empty.

Three undated sightings cap our file on cougars. Witness "Lisa" of Springfield filed her report in October 2010, saying she saw a cougar "years ago," on Spring Gap Road in Levels.[114] In April 2011, Traci Luikart wrote that her father had seen cougars "on several occasions" near Hurricane (Putnam County).[115] Finally, an undated report from Don Woods recalled seeing a cougar near Gormania (Grant County) "about six years ago." Don's wife had also seen one near Lead Mine (Tucker County) "about three years ago."[116]

I leave the reader to decide if DNR denials should be trusted, or if cougars still roam West Virginia's wilderness. ■

>> JET BLACK

MORE PUZZLING THAN COUGAR SIGHTINGS, by far, are reports of "black panthers" in West Virginia. Technically speaking, no such cats exist, but the name is commonly applied both to melanistic jaguars (*Panthera onca*) and leopards (*Panthera pardus*). Cryptozoologists sometimes refer to melanistic cougars, but despite anecdotal reports dating back to the mid-eighteenth century, no black cougar has ever been killed or captured. Reports of large black cats, then, must refer to something else.

Panther sightings are a relatively new phenomenon in West Virginia. While some US regions claim reports dating from pre-Columbian times, the Mountain State's first sighting occurred at Hinton (Summers County) on June 15, 1949. Constable Jesse Romanello was on patrol at 11:45 p.m., when his headlights framed "a black animal from fifteen to eighteen inches high and about four feet long exclusive of the long slim tail, which was carried with

an up-curl at the end." It fled into the woods, leaving Romanello to surmise that it "might have escaped from a road show somewhere near," but no such escapes were reported.[117]

February 1951 witnessed a panther flap in Charleston, as authorities hunted the "Black Devil of Coal Branch Heights," described as a beast that was "black and shaggy and stood about waist high." J. H. Branham, speaking for the state's Conservation Commission—forerunner of the DNR—denied there were any panthers at large, suggesting that the Devil might be a "stray bear." Similar cases were reported "almost every year," he said. "The animals, we find, are either vicious dogs or some small game strayed away from its home." Vigilantes joined the hunt, in vain.[118]

Mrs. Holland Vernon reported a panther sighting from Hepzibah (Harrison County) on July 25, 1960, prompting another fruitless search. Five years later, in June 1965, residents of North Charleston rallied to hunt yet another black panther. Witnesses said, "It was pretty big, had a long tail and a face like a cat." Again, the prowler managed to escape.[119]

Point Pleasant (Mason County)—best known for appearances of "Mothman" (Chapter 4), later plagued by a "werewolf" (Chapter 3)—suffered a spate of panther sightings in September 1978. As usual, the jet-black cougar-sized cat eluded pursuers, vanishing as mysteriously as it appeared.[120]

Witness "B. Foster" logged the next panther sighting in June 1979 or '80, at Horner (Lewis County). En route to Stonecoal Lake with a cousin, Foster saw the cat, initially mistaking it for a black German Shepherd, until he noted that "the ears looked really strange and small and the face seemed short." Locals scoffed at his story, but Foster says "it wasn't too long [before] others saw it."[121]

An anonymous e-mail correspondent, writing in February 2010, personally questioned the existence of black panthers in the Mountain State, then wrote, "but I have family here in Elkview [Kanawha County] and back in the early '80s they have seen black ones, and heard the screaming like a woman sounds. They told us as kids to not to go into the woods if we heard such a sound."[122]

Witness "Rachel" also wrote, in September 2010: "We used to see black panthers in the '80s quite frequently but had not seen any for many years. Our dogs have been going crazy at night and won't go anywhere away from the house and I had a dog come up missing recently."[123]

While bow hunting in 1985, James Bergstrom and his brother met "a large, completely black mountain lion" on a logging trail near Old Stony Dam in Grant County. The cat's appearance shocked them and spooked a deer they were stalking.[124]

E-mail correspondent "Falco" cannot recall if his Parkersburg panther sighting occurred in 1988 or '89. At 3 a.m. on the summer night in question, he had finished fishing with friends on the Little Kanawha River, across from the Corning-Schott Scientific Glass plant, and was headed home when "a HUGE cat," four feet long excluding its tail, leaped onto the roadway. During the brief encounter, Falco noted that "its tail was very thick, heavy looking, black with a rounded tip, quite long also."[125]

"Tom H." was driving through Lincoln County on Route 34, near Harvey Creek, when he saw "a cougar-sized black cat" lounging atop a roadside woodpile, sometime in 1988 or '89. He questioned his own perception, finally reporting the encounter in 2009, after reading other reports of panthers at large.[126] John Lutz, writing in 1989, ranked West Virginia third among fifteen eastern states reporting panthers, with twenty-nine sightings logged since 1983.[127]

Witness "Ronnie S." saw a panther in 1990, while dropping off a trailer at a Webster County coal mine on Gauley River Road. He described it as six to seven feet long, tail included, "with a big head with small ears, black shiny hair with a long bushy tail." Its pawprints measured 4½ inches wide.[128]

In 1992 or '93, trucker "J. Gore" met a panther near Sharples (Logan County). His headlights suddenly illuminated shining eyes, and then he saw "a LARGE black cat" crouched on the pavement, its long tail "switching back and forth like a house cat would when annoyed." A moment later, bolting into nearby woods, the panther disappeared.[129]

Correspondent "Carla," writing in July 2004, reports that her father, two brothers, and several friends met a panther in Greenbrier County, while hunting rabbits in January 1998. The party's tracking dogs flushed "a large black creature...much too large to be a dog." It ran "at an incredible rate of speed," pausing to snarl and bare its fangs until the dogs turned tail.[130]

John and Linda Lutz updated their statistics

on panther sightings in October 2001, citing seventy-six eyewitness reports from West Virginia between July 1983 and December 2000. This time, the state ranked fifth in sightings, behind Pennsylvania, New York, Wisconsin, and Maryland.[131]

An anonymous witness from Pocahontas County, writing to the Gulf Coast Bigfoot Research Organization in May 2003, reported three Bigfoot sightings (see Chapter 8), then added: "This may seem just as odd. In the area of the nighttime sighting there has been over twenty sightings of a huge (over three hundred pound) BLACK mountain lion. I have found tracks the size of a gallon coffee can lid up until May 5, 2003, when I looked across the road and saw a long black thing sticking up (its tail) then like a cat catching mice it leaped about ten feet out of the brush and then disappeared in the laurel thicket."[132]

Two days before that sighting, Josh Kyer reported his own encounter with a panther on the Cherry River, near Richwood (Nicholas County). Camped with his father, Kyer heard twigs snapping around 2 a.m. and peered from his tent to see "a long and slender black cat that was about four or five feet long and a massive tail." He watched the beast for five minutes or more, clearly visible in light from Kyer's campfire.[133]

In January 2005, Pendleton County farmer Jason Brown caught an apparent black panther on videotape in broad daylight. The History Channel aired his tape on its *MonsterQuest* program, in December 2007, including expert analysis of the video stating that the animal depicted measured 24.92 inches from its nose to the base of its tail—6.82 inches longer than the average house cat. The difference was marginal, however, and the show's producers would not call the video hard proof of panthers in the Mountain State.[134]

Another off-topic report on panthers reached the GCBRO's website in February 2011. The correspondent shared two stories from

THE ONLY "BLACK PANTHERS"
RECOGNIZED BY SCIENCE ARE
MELANISTIC LEOPARDS (LIKE
THIS ONE) OR JAGUARS.

relatives, spanning half a century. In one case, during 1956, her grandfather and brother met a panther on a swinging bridge, while making rural merchandise deliveries. The second incident, involving the correspondent's mother, described a "big black cat" killing a fawn, while two black cubs looked on.[135]

In July 2009, a Ritchie County witness reported a possible Bigfoot encounter to the Bigfoot Field Researchers Organization (BFRO). That report mentioned in passing that the witness "was armed as there are wild dogs, bears, and a black panther running round back here."[136] Sadly, he included no further information on the mysterious cat.

In early spring 2007, while hiking through Cranberry Glades with her husband, Melodie Spencer saw a panther cross their path. Woman and cat briefly regarded one another, then the panther retreated. Spencer's husband missed the cat, but saw its pawprints in the snow.[137]

On August 29, 2008, while driving through Preston County on Cranesville Road, Sue Maund saw a panther race across the pavement. She compared its size to her own German Shepherd, around eighty pounds. "The tail was as long as the body and was thick," she wrote. "Its back feet were large. I did not see much more than that. It was booking across the road, two leaps and it was gone. I know it was no domestic cat, due to the way it moved and the size."[138]

On November 19, 2008, animal control officer Mary Daggett met three panthers while driving on Route 18 South, near Porto Rico (Doddridge County). The pride consisted of "a HUGE cat with two smaller ones," Daggett wrote, adding that "practically everyone on this road has seen them at least once. I've seen them twice more on our farm, one neighbor saw one right outside her backdoor, and they've been seen crossing the road, slinking across fields, etc."[139]

Witness "Shawn" reported an atypical sighting of "a snow-white panther" in Logan County, on February 14, 2009. Records exist of white cougars, either albino or leucistic (with pigmented skin and eyes), but Shawn's report added another twist: "I have also watched black panthers come down when it's very quiet out, on Sunday mornings."[140]

Samantha Dickinson saw a panther on April 1, 2009, stressing that her report was "not a prank." Driving on US Route 19 at 7:45 a.m., between Fayetteville and Summersville, she saw several cars stopped and did likewise, observing the cat as it strolled on the highway's median.[141]

On April 17, Jeremy Pelter and his wife met a panther on State Route 93, in Tucker County. "It moved like a lion," he wrote, "and had a long tail that extended from the end of its back almost to the ground."[142]

One month later, at 8:30 p.m. on May nineteenth, William Rhodes and his sons returned home from a Boy Scouts meeting in Walton (Roane County) to find a panther in their garden. It fled as Rhodes entered the driveway, but he suspected it of snatching the family's cat.[143]

At 11 a.m. on July 6, 2009, Dwayne Atkins saw a panther descending a hillside along Interstate 77 near Chelyan (Kanawha County). He pegged its weight around 200 pounds, adding, "It appeared to be after a dead animal in the ditch."[144] The same day brought a sighting from Highway 33 near Elkins, where Brad Christian saw "a large black cat running in the short grass at the side of the road. It wasn't in a hurry so we had a lot of time to see it. It was far too large to be a domestic cat and had a large long full tail."[145]

In August 2009, Cynthia Lawson logged a Braxton County report dating from her childhood. Her brother had seen a panther while walking to work, and Lawson herself heard a cat's banshee screams near her Wirt County home. Years later, when she and her friends described the cats to a college professor, "he thought we were full of it."[146] Witness "Rachel" reports that her cousin was walking his dogs on Wills Creek, in Elkview, when a panther interrupted their stroll on September 1, 2010.[147]

The GCBRO received its third West Virginia panther report on May 1, 2011, describing a Wayne County sighting on April 5. An anonymous witness saw the cat from his back porch, around 9:15 a.m., adding that other black cats had confronted an uncle and cousin during recent months.[148] In summer 2011, Jadyn Phillips was feeding horses at his home near Thornton (Taylor County), when he turned to see "an oddly large cougar" with "a mysterious jet black coat" watching from its seat on a nearby log. The cat stared at Phillips for roughly ten minutes, then melted into the forest.[149]

Correspondent "Erin B." reported a spate of panther sightings to Cougar Quest in March 2012. A Mercer County resident glimpsed a "giant black cat" from her window in daylight, on March 22, while "others have seen and heard" panthers, reporting slaughter of chickens, cats, and dogs. A similar report—in fact, verbatim—issued from Berkeley County on March 31.[150]

Another belated childhood report of panther sightings emerged in May 2012, from Pocahontas County. Iva Williams, then age seventy, recalled an incident from March 1950, near Kennison Mountain. One night, a beast came prowling around the family's home, and Iva looked outside to see "this big ole, black cat sittin' on the bench clawin' at the window." Raising a lamp, she frightened it away.[151]

Lewanna Warner's mother phoned her from McWhorter (Harrison County) on May 15, 2012, reporting her daylight encounter with "a big cat of some type...It was black with a thick, long black tail that drags the ground and flips up once in a while."[152]

Two months later, at 1:30 a.m. on July 23rd, Brittany Lewis glimpsed a panther from her porch, prowling a nearby hill. "I noticed a little white spot on its chest," she wrote, "and how long its tail was. The whole cat was about ten feet long and to its shoulder was the height of a black panther." In a macabre twist, Lewis adds that when she ran indoors, she fell and cut her lip. Moments later, she peered outside and saw the cat on her porch, lapping up her spilled blood.[153]

Our last panther report, so far, comes from clinical psychologist Lucy Kirby. On January 15, 2013, she wrote: "I have spent countless hours and even weeks in the mountains backpacking. I have seen several mountain lions especially in Pocahontas County and on Dolly Sods [Wilderness, part of the Monongahela National Forest]. I tracked and watched one black cat for two years. I called her Pandora because of her nature...I know what I saw and have been tracking them for twenty years."[154] ∎

KING OF BEASTS

IF PANTHERS IN WEST VIRGINIA boggle the mind, what should we make of "African" lion sightings? *Panthera leo* is the second largest living cat, after the tiger (*Panthera tigris*), once found from Greece to India, where a subspecies still survives in the Gir Forest National Park. A Pleistocene ancestor, *P. l. atrox*, once roamed freely from the Yukon to Peru, but scientists assure us that the species disappeared 10,000 years ago.

In *Mysterious America,* author Loren Coleman mentions a West Virginia lion sighting from 1836, but the report is clearly in error. He places the "maned, roaring" cat in Penobscot County (actually found in Maine), and a cross-reference to Chapter 3 reveals no mention of lions or West Virginia.[155]

Next up, we have the following report from folklorist Henry Wharton Shoemaker:

> The hide of a West Virginia pantheress killed on the Greenbriar [sic] River, Poca- hontas County, in 1901, three-quarters grown, owned by Hon. C. K. Sober, of Lewisburg, has long white hair on chest and belly, a fluffy, dark brown tail, culmi- nating in a large tuft of black hair, like the tip of the tail of an African lion. It measured seven feet three inches from tip to tip.[156]

In fact, the tail's tuft proves the cat was not a "pantheress." Only lions have that feature, which conceals a spur approximately one-fifth of an inch in length, formed by fusion of the tailbone's final segments. Absent at birth, the tuft sprouts around five months of age and is clearly visible at seven months, on both males and females.[157]

Clearly, then, at least one lioness was on the prowl in West Virginia during 1901. More than a century later, in October 2007, an aged Greenbrier County bow hunter reported his encounter with a male of the species. "It had a mane," he told the Beckley *Daily Mail,* "so I could tell it was male. And I'm sure it wasn't a bear. Bears are all over Cold Knob. I see six to eight of them every time I go hunting, and I can tell the difference. Bears don't shake me up at all. This lion made me pretty nervous." Nonetheless, he watched it for forty minutes, later reporting the incident to DNR agents. They told him his was the county's second lion sighting.[158]

The latter case may be explained, in theory, by release of an exotic pet by some irresponsible owner. West Virginia's law is lax in regard to exotic creatures. It states: "The [DNR's] director may issue a permit to a person to keep and maintain in captivity as a pet, a wild animal or wild bird that has been acquired from a commercial dealer or during the legal open season. The fee therefor shall be two dollars."[159] As for unlicensed pets, their number and location is unknown until some tragedy occurs, bringing police down on the lawbreakers. ■

"AFRICAN" LIONS ONCE INHABITED MOST OF THE OLD WORLD AND STILL SURVIVE IN PARTS OF INDIA.

Credit: Dantheman9758 at the English language Wikipedia

ARTIST'S RECONSTRUCTION OF PANTHERA LEO ATROX, PRESUMED EXTINCT FOR 10,000 YEARS.

>> ONE OF A KIND?

LOREN COLEMAN AND COLLEAGUE MARK HALL suggest an answer both for lion and black panther sightings in America: they propose that *P. l. atrox* has survived into modern times. Males of the species—standing four feet high at the shoulder, measuring up to eight feet from nose to the base of the tail, weighing 770 pounds—might thus account for sightings of maned "African" lions prowling North American fields and forests. Coleman and Hall further suggest that females of the species are prone to sexual dimorphism, producing melanistic specimens.[160]

Voilà! Two mysteries solved at once—or, are they?

Some eyewitness reports appear to support that theory. During August 1948, multiple sightings from Ohio and Indiana described a large maned cat traveling with a black panther and a tawny lioness. In 1964, a maned cat and a panther visited Will County, Illinois. In 1986, a maned cat and a striped companion roamed at will over four Pennsylvania counties.[161]

That said, three problems dog the theory raised by Hall and Coleman. First, science insists that *P. l. atrox* has been extinct for ten millennia. Second, most reconstructions of the species from fossils depict male specimens without a mane. And finally, no evidence of melanistic females presently exists. The rest is tantalizing speculation, leading...nowhere. ∎

MORE TIGERS ARE FOUND IN CAPTIVITY IN THE UNITED STATES THAN IN THE WILD WORLDWIDE.

Credit: US Fish & Wildlife Service

STRIPES AND SOLIDS

IF LIONS AND PANTHERS PROWL WEST VIRGINIA, why not tigers? The largest living cat may top eleven feet in length and weigh more than 850 pounds. Six subspecies, all endangered, range from India through Southeast Asia to Siberia; three others are officially extinct. None should exist outside captivity in North America. And yet...

John Lutz reports that crewmen aboard Train No. 62 saw a large, striped cat near Spruce Knob, in Cass Scenic Railroad State Park, one afternoon in June 1977. The witnesses described brown stripes, but failed to note the felid's background color, which may range from reddish-orange to white in tigers. Stripes may be pale or dark. This particular tiger—if tiger it was—reportedly ran across the track in plain view of an engineer and fireman, then vanished in the woods.[162]

Before speculating on tigers breeding at large in West Virginia, we should recall the state's lax regulation of exotic pets. In 2012, authorities counted 5,000 captive tigers in the United States, versus 3,200 living free worldwide.[163] The World Wildlife Fund and other organizations seek to end the global traffic in exotic cats, but they receive little support from states where two dollars procures a license to collect large predators.

Another long-shot possibility harks back to Hall and Coleman's theory of relict American lions surviving today. Some reconstructions of those cats depict them with lightly striped or spotted coats—although, again, fossils provide no evidence of coloration in a living specimen. ■

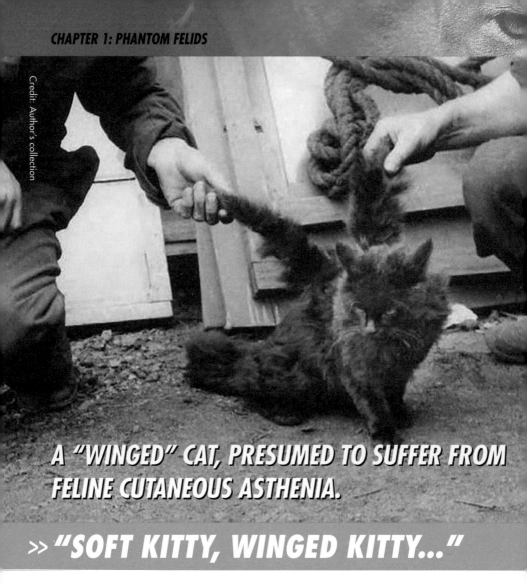

Credit: Author's collection

A "WINGED" CAT, PRESUMED TO SUFFER FROM FELINE CUTANEOUS ASTHENIA.

>> "SOFT KITTY, WINGED KITTY..."

IN MAY OF 1959, young Douglas Shelton's dog treed a peculiar creature in the woods outside Pineville. Shelton nearly shot the animal before he recognized it as a cat—with wings! Climbing to seize the cat, who offered no resistance, Shelton took it home and named it Thomas, then began to charge his neighbors ten cents each to view his pet. The news soon reached Fern Miniacs, a reporter with the *Beckley Post-Herald*, who recognized "Thomas" as a female Persian. Miniacs also determined that the cat's "wings" were composed of gristle, but no bone.

That finding barely fazed the public. On June 8, 1959, Thomas and Shelton appeared as featured guests on NBC's *Today Show*. Watching, back in Pineville, Mrs. Charles Hicks recognized Thomas, proclaiming that "he" was, in fact, her lost cat Mitzi, who had run away from home four days prior to being captured by Shelton. Hicks demanded return of her pet, Shelton refused, and Hicks filed suit in court. At trial, on October 5th, Shelton appeared with a wingless Persian and two clumps of matted fur in a shoebox, declaring that Thomas had shed her "wings" in July.

Mrs. Hicks cried foul, receiving a judgment of one dollar in damages, while Shelton retained custody of Thomas.[164]

No one ever claimed Thomas could fly, though a similar cat allegedly did—and was shot from midair by a frightened Ontario confectioner—seven years later, in June 1966.[165] Worldwide, at least 138 "winged" cats have been reported since 1842; thirty cases are documented with physical evidence, including twenty photos and a video.[166]

Veterinarians often attribute feline "wings" to feline cutaneous asthenia, a disease related to Ehlers-Danlos syndrome ("elastic skin") in humans. Both ailments result from defects in the structure, production, or processing of collagen, causing incurable mutations whose severity may range from mild to life threatening. In other cases, the "wings" may be matted hair in dire need of trimming. Neither should permit a cat to fly—unless we believe that candy maker in Ontario. ■

CHAPTER 2

IN COLD BLOOD

Herpetologists acknowledge eighty-seven species of reptiles and amphibians living wild in modern West Virginia. They include thirteen turtle species, six lizards, twenty snakes, thirty-four salamanders, and fourteen frogs and toads.[1] All are poikilotherms—commonly called "cold-blooded"—creatures whose internal temperature and activity level varies with the ambient temperature of their environment. Two species definitely not included, but reported nonetheless, are giant snakes and alligators.

AMERICAN ALLIGATORS DO NOT OCCUR NATURALLY IN WEST VIRGINIA.

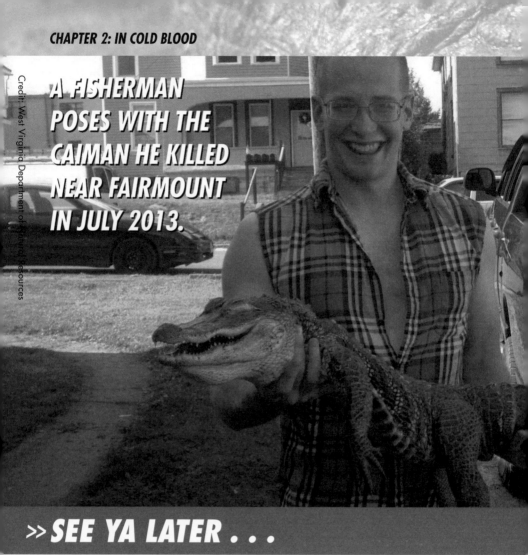

Credit: West Virginia Department of Natural Resources

A FISHERMAN POSES WITH THE CAIMAN HE KILLED NEAR FAIRMOUNT IN JULY 2013.

>> SEE YA LATER . . .

CROCODILIANS ARE REPRESENTED in North America by the American alligator (*Alligator mississippiensis*) and the American crocodile (*Crocodylus acutus*). In the United States, *C. acutus* is restricted to the southern tip of Florida. Alligators have a wider range, but still should not encroach on West Virginia. Their nearest recognized outpost lies in Dare County, North Carolina, some 270 miles from the Mountain State's eastern border.[2] The trek from there should be impossible—and lethal, during winter—yet gators and their kin keep showing up where they do not belong.

Jack Stonestreet was fishing along Lincoln County's Upper Mud River on October 7, 2010, when an alligator paddled past him. "I didn't even tell my wife," Stonestreet said later, "because, to be honest, I didn't think anyone would believe me." Other fisherman glimpsed the reptile, as well, reporting their encounters to the DNR. On October 9th, field supervisor Nick Huffman saw the animal himself. "I would say he's a half grown alligator, a total measurement of sixty-seven inches," he said. "That's big enough I knew not to get on him in hand-to-hand combat." Instead, he summoned marksmen to kill the gator, telling reporters it would be dissected in search of "some insight as to where it may have come from and how long it was in the river." No further word was forthcoming.[3]

On June 21, 2011, a driver traveling on Teays Valley Road near St. Albans (Putnam County) swerved to miss an alligator in the middle of the highway, winding up stuck in a ditch. Sheriff's deputies captured the reptile and delivered it to DNR Corporal Gary Amick, who ordered it shot after Marshall University declined to accept it. Amick speculated that some local resident had bought the gator while vacationing in South Carolina or Florida. "People bring them home thinking 'this is so cute' and put it in an aquarium," he told the Charleston Gazette, "but then when it grows to be three foot long in a five-gallon aquarium, it becomes too much to handle. They don't want to kill it, because it's their pet, so they'll turn it loose thinking it'll find its way back to the wild."[4]

DNR wildlife chief Curtis Taylor professed ignorance of his state's law concerning exotic species. "There are species referred to as injurious," he said, "such as the northern snakehead fish, and those species are regulated by the US Fish and Wildlife Service. It's against federal law to bring those species in. Some of the more poisonous snakes are on that list. Alligators are not on the federal list. We defer to federal law on dangerous or injurious species, but to my knowledge, our state law has nothing against exotics."[5]

Indeed, as we have seen, an alligator may be licensed for two dollars, if its owner cares to bother.

The next stray gator—a three-foot-long specimen—surfaced in Burlington on July 25, 2012. DNR agents pulled it from a sewer, aided by an unnamed Ohio State Highway Patrol officer whose presence at the scene, eighty miles outside his legal jurisdiction, remains unexplained. This time, the reptile was taken alive, transported to the DNR's regional office, where a spokesman told reporters officers would "wait and hear if the gator's owner tries to contact them before they send it somewhere else."[6] Again, no follow-up was published.

On April 25, 2013, landscapers found a thirty-inch alligator standing guard over their equipment at Wildflower Creek Estates, outside Martinsburg. They summoned a neighbor to wrangle the reptile, and he called Berkeley County sheriff's deputies. They, in turn, summoned the state police and DNR to deal with the disgruntled six-pound reptile. "They all converged on this place kind of like at one time," witness Robert Maraugha told reporters. "It looks like it's well fed. I don't have any clue. There's hasn't been any notices like lost alligator, nothing like that. Why of all places in West Virginia this thing turned up in my backyard is beyond my scope of understanding." Once again, officials blamed negligent owners and the gator vanished from the public record.[7]

DNR agents should have known that crocodilians are readily available in pet stores statewide. On July 15, 2013, thieves stole a foot-long juvenile alligator valued at $300 from a pet store in Beckley. The thief was caught on videotape but remains unidentified. Proprietor Anthony Williams did not miss the reptile until feeding time, the next morning.[8]

Three months later, on October 4, two fishermen caught and killed another crocodilian, while trolling on the Monongahela River between Fairmont and Rivesville. That unfortunate beast was a caiman (genus Caiman), closely related to alligators. Three living species are native to Central and South America, ranging from three to thirteen feet in length at maturity, but the Monongahela River caiman was not formally identified.[9] Presumably, it was another "pet" abandoned by a callous, foolish owner. ∎

>> *SNAKES IN THE GRASS*

Credit: US Fish & Wildlife Service

THE NORTHERN PINE SNAKE IS WEST VIRGINIA'S LARGEST KNOWN SNAKE SPECIES.

WEST VIRGINIA'S TWENTY SNAKE SPECIES include five of fairly large size. The northern pine snake (*Pituophis melanoleucus melanoleucus*), with a record length of eight feet four inches, is officially the champion. The black rat snake (*Elaphe obsoleta obsoleta*) boasts a record of six feet eight inches. The longest confirmed timber rattlesnake (*Crotalus horridus*) measured six feet two inches, while the record northern black racer (*Coluber constrictor constrictor*) was one inch shorter. The corn snake (*Elaphe guttata guttata*) may reach six feet, and the eastern black king snake (*Lampropeltis getula* ssp.) claims a record of five feet four inches.[10]

Any of the five are large enough to terrify an ophidiophobe, but none qualify as giants,

a term reserved by herpetologists for certain members of the families Boidae and Pythonidae—the boas, anacondas, and pythons. Such giants do exist in the United States, courtesy of the exotic pet trade, and authorities have confirmed two large python species, *Python bivittatus* and *P. sebae*, breeding wild in southern Florida.[11] A female python with a nest of eggs was also found in Texas, in October 2009.[12]

No such giants have been caught roaming through modern West Virginia, but reports of giant snakes at large date from the midnineteenth century. In April 1884, David Baker met a huge serpent at Knottville, two miles from Grafton. The snake escaped when Baker ran to fetch his gun from home, but

CORN SNAKES RANK AS WEST VIRGINIA'S FOURTH-LARGEST RECOGNIZED SNAKE SPECIES.

Credit: US Fish & Wildlife Service

he described it as "about fourteen feet long and of a dirty clay color. It was as thick as a man's waist and because of its size its head was raised about two feet above the ground."[13]

While startling in itself, the snake's appearance was not new to Taylor County residents. Newspaper reports dated its first sighting from 1854, with other reports in 1874 and 1882. According to the press:

All of these different tales agree as to the appearance of the monster except that when he was first seen, thirty years ago, he was but ten feet long. The inhabitants along the swamp express their fixed determination to capture the beast dead or alive. They have found its den and will watch until the snake makes his appearance.[14]

That stakeout failed, no great surprise considering the snake had managed to survive fifty West Virginia winters, with temperatures near or below freezing. Then again, if other native reptiles and amphibians can hibernate, why not a giant?

Two years after the Taylor County snake scare, Melzer Braley met a very different monster on Big Two Mile Creek near Milton (Cabell County). Braley was passing a cave known to locals as the Buzzard Den, when he heard a sheep bleating inside. Following the sound, he saw a snake "forty feet long, with black and yellow stripes running

A BURMESE PYTHON, ONCE SOMEONE'S PET, FOUND LIVING WILD IN FLORIDA.

THE NORTHERN BLACK RACER MAY EXCEED SIX FEET IN LENGTH.

THE EASTERN BLACK KING SNAKE (NOT ENTIRELY BLACK) IS THE SMALLEST OF WEST VIRGINIA'S RELATIVELY LARGE SNAKE SPECIES.

A TIMBER RATTLESNAKE, WEST VIRGINIA'S LARGEST VENOMOUS SPECIES, DOES NOT RESEMBLE DIAMONDBACK RATTLERS.

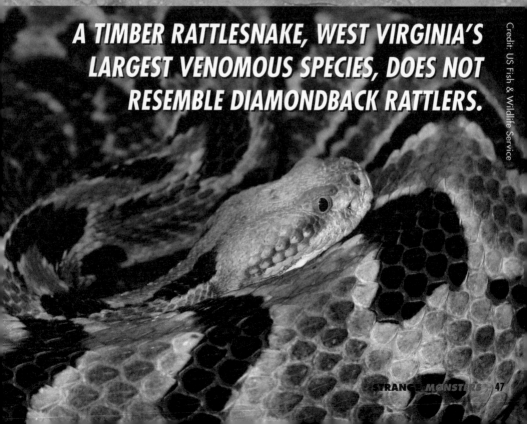

Credit: US Fish & Wildlife Service

A MELANISTIC TIMBER RATTLER CLEARLY DISPLAYS NO "DIAMONDBACK" PATTERN.

lengthwise of its body," swallowing the hapless sheep hindquarters first. Bounding up the hillside, Braley rolled a large stone down upon the serpent, which released its prey and fled. Braley did likewise, but returned with reinforcements. According to a newspaper report, "the snake was not seen again, although its hissing could be heard coming from within the cave."[15]

Our next press account of a huge snake at large, in September 1889, is lamentably brief: "There is a story going the rounds about a monster snake which is supposed to have been seen near Mount de Chantal Academy, near Wheeling, at various times recently. It is described as being about twenty feet long and as thick as a man's body."[16] Mount de

Chantal, a private Catholic school, remained in operation until 2008, but nothing more is known of its resident reptile.

Our last report of an oversized serpent comes from Hamlin, in Lincoln County. There, sometime in 1936, one Bernie Skeens allegedly killed a rattlesnake measuring "a mite over fourteen feet long." With the head and its twenty-eight rattles removed, the snake's skin still measured twelve feet, seven inches in length. Tacked to the wall of a local smokehouse, the hide was viewed and described—but, sadly, not photographed—by Adrian Gwin, a reporter for the Charleston *Daily Mail*, in October 1954. The smokehouse later burned, and no trace of the hide remains today.[17]

BLACK RAT SNAKES MAY REACH A LENGTH OF SIX FEET, EIGHT INCHES.

Hamlin residents referred to the late giant as a "black diamondback," displaying a "normal" forty-two-inch specimen's skin next to the monster's, for comparison. No such species is known to science: West Virginia's only rattlesnake is the timber rattler, which may be black but never displays a "diamondback" pattern. No true diamondbacks—eastern (*Crotalus adamanteus*), red (*C. ruber*), or western (*C. atrox*)—naturally occur in West Virginia or any neighboring states.

Snake skins, whether shed or forcibly removed, should not be trusted to supply the donor's length. A hide may stretch substantially during the tanning process—some sources claim up to thirty percent—which could reduce the living Logan County giant to eight feet ten inches, plus its missing head and rattles. That still exceeds the timber rattler's official record by two feet seven inches, and tops the longest confirmed eastern diamondback by a foot.

So, what was it? What were any of the giants seen in West Virginia?

It is conceivable, barely, that large exotic snakes may have been smuggled in during the nineteenth century, for some unknown purpose, but the specimens described from Taylor and Cabell Counties resemble no python, boa or anaconda known to modern science. Like the huge "black diamondback," they live today only in rumor and in mystery. ■

CHAPTER 3

GOING TO THE DOGS

West Virginia once harbored four native species of the family Canidae, which includes coyotes, dogs, foxes, jackals, and wolves. As in the case of cougars, eastern timber wolves (*Canis lupus lycaon*) were hunted ruthlessly, with bounties offered for their "scalps" through the late nineteenth century, until a Randolph County hunter shot the state's last known specimen in January 1900. The DNR explains sporadic sightings from the hinterlands as pets released by owners, or by claiming that the creatures seen are other members of the canine family.

Credit: US Fish & Wildlife Service

STATE OFFICIALS
RANK COYOTES AS
UNCOMMON, DUE TO
HUNTING AND HABITAT
DESTRUCTION.

Credit: US Fish & Wildlife Service

EASTERN TIMBER WOLVES WERE OFFICIALLY EXTIRPATED FROM WEST VIRGINIA IN 1900.

Surviving canids in the Mountain State include the gray fox (*Urocyon cinereoargenteus*) and red fox (*Vulpes vulpes*), both rated as "common" by DNR spokesmen, and coyotes (*Canis latrans*), ranked as "uncommon" due to habitat destruction and natural secretive habits. Coyotes are the largest of the native canids, measuring up to fifty inches from nose to tail tip, standing around two feet high at the shoulder. Feral domestic dogs (*Canis lupus familiaris*), considered an exotic species, may be any size, from a Chihuahua to a Great Dane, and may complicate our survey of West Virginia's cryptic canids. ■

>> DEMON DOG OR DEMON RUM?

OUR FIRST REPORT of a ravenous canid at large comes from Monroe County, dated sometime in the 1880s. Witness Ellis Sparr's account of the event is tainted by his notorious alcoholism, which prompted accusations that he often neglected his wife and six children.

One October night, after work, Sparr rode his mare Nell six miles from home to Sweet Springs, along a dirt track that is now State Route 3. Returning home well in his cups, by moonlight, Spar saw a large black animal approaching on a roadside bank, initially believing that it was his family's dog. Pleasure turned to shock, however, when the beast leaped down upon Nell's flanks, behind Sparr's saddle, snarling like a rabid fiend.

Drunk and befuddled, close to panic, Sparr flailed at the attacker, later reporting that he felt "nothing but air" when striking it. Nell had a better plan, galloping on toward home, eventually shaking off her tormentor, escaping any major injury. Starr reached the threshold of his home "stone sober," though accounts of the incident's aftermath differ: some claim he gave up drinking attack; others say he consumed more booze than ever before.[1]

Sparr's encounter occurred while eastern gray wolves still survived in West Virginia, but no attacks by wolves on humans have been documented in the Mountain State. In fact, only twenty-nine attacks have been confirmed from all of North America, from 1820 to 2013. Of those, eleven occurred in Alaska, ten in Canada, three in Minnesota, with one each in California, Colorado, Kentucky, New Jersey, and North Dakota.[2] ■

THE MONSTER OF MORGAN RIDGE

IN 1929, immigrant Frank Kozul lived at Fairmount (Marion County), and worked nearby, at a mine owned by the Consolidated Coal Company. The mine is located on Morgan Ridge Road, known at the time for a ferocious monster said to prowl the area. One night, after his shift, Kozul took a shortcut through the woods and met that creature in the flesh.

According to his description, the beast was canine in form, two feet tall at the shoulder, and cloaked in white hair, with a large head and a bushy tail. After snarling at Kozul, it leaped for his throat and he swung his lunch pail in self-defense—but like Ellis Sparr before him, struck only thin air. The hellhound had sufficient heft to stagger Kozul, but he kept his footing and escaped, pursued for several hundred yards with the creature snapping and snarling behind him, its foul odor filling his nostrils. Only when he reached a rural graveyard did the monster vanish as mysteriously as it had appeared, leaving its victim terrified but physically unharmed.[3] ■

HELLHOUNDS

OTHER CANINE CREATURES in the Mountain State are more substantial than the beasts encountered by Sparr and Kozul. On July 14, 2004, cousins Jeff Ward and Allen Peyatt posted a report online, describing an event that occurred "on or about November 23rd [of] the year I cannot remember." They were at a deer hunter's camp on Cranberry Ridge (Webster County), when their adult companions sent them to fetch lard for cooking the midday meal. Mounting an ATV, Ward and Peyatt reached the Gauley River, then a hard rain fell and mired their four-wheeler in mud.

While grappling with their vehicle and waiting for the rain to pass, Ward saw "what appeared to be a huge wolf standing on its hind legs behind us on the path. All I could

Credit: US National Oceanic and Atmospheric Administration

THE GAULEY RIVER, SCENE OF A PURPORTED "WEREWOLF" SIGHTING.

see was a silhouette but the first thing I thought was WEREWOLF...It had a long snout and long pointy ears and stood at least 6½ feet tall. It was all hairy and very intimidating."[4]

Terrified, the boys gunned their ATV and fled at top speed to a relative's home, where they persuaded her to load the four-wheeler in her pickup truck and drive them back to camp. On arrival, Ward wrote, "Everyone at camp wondered why we did not ride back on the ATV. When we told them, they thought we were making it up. To this day, none believes us."[5]

A similar "demon creature" haunted Lincoln County in the spring of 1980, this one leaving slaughtered livestock in its wake. An anonymous blogger, writing a quarter century later, recalled his brother's encounter with the beast near their grandmother's home in

Yawkey, while strolling with his fiancée. According to that account:

My brother has hunted all of his life and is familiar with all the indigenous species in these woods, but he says that he has never seen anything like what stood before them that day. It was a large black-furred animal that was larger than a bear, and had a long bushy tail and pointed snout similar to a wolf. When it first stepped on the trail it was walking on all fours. My brother says that it had a foul odor, and the very site of it made his hair stand on end...When it stepped on the trail it suddenly came to a stop, stood up on its hind legs like a man, and then turned and stared at them. My brother says its eyes were small, and shone bright neon red. When

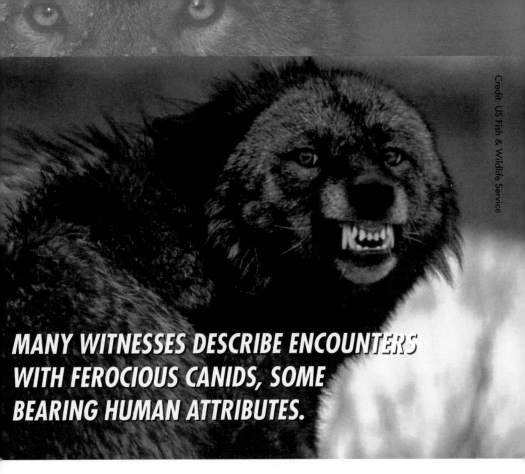

MANY WITNESSES DESCRIBE ENCOUNTERS WITH FEROCIOUS CANIDS, SOME BEARING HUMAN ATTRIBUTES.

it stood on its hind legs, he said that it easily stood seven feet tall. His heart sank when it turned and looked at them—he knew for sure that they were dead. But then it walked off the very steep side of the mountain to the right of trail, still standing on its hind legs. He says that it didn't stand like a bear, but almost as if it was meant to be walking on its hind legs, which were somewhat larger and longer than its front arms or legs.[6]

The witness told relatives of the incident, prompting his father to recall events from his own childhood in the 1930s and '40s. A similar beast paid occasional visits, he said, emitting a foul odor and frightening fierce hunting dogs. On mornings after its nocturnal visits, locals would emerge from hiding to the sight of mangled cows or horses. "To this day," the blogger wrote, "nobody has ever been able to tell exactly what this thing is, but many have reported having encounters with it."[7]

Email correspondent "Sylvia" resides in West Virginia's Northern Panhandle, formerly Virginia's Yohogania County, now consisting of four smaller counties sandwiched between Pennsylvania and Ohio. Writing in December 2005, she said:

Since I was a kid, we've heard rumors that an unknown beast has lived in some wooded areas near my home. It has the same description of similar sightings and what not, except we don't think it's a Bigfoot. Those who have seen the alleged beast said it ran like a dog, and seems to be carnivorous...There were several dogs missing and some of them came up half eaten in the woods.[8]

AN ANCIENT EUROPEAN WOODCUT OF VILLAGERS HUNTING WEREWOLVES.

Eight months after that account was posted online, in August 2006, witness "Irving" from Elkins saw a frightening quasi-canid beast in the Dolly Sods Wilderness. As he described the incident:

> It started to rain so I was heading back toward my truck. On my way I noticed something big move out of some thickets about fifty yards to my left. I stopped to get a better look with my binoculars. I waited until I saw more movement then aimed the binoculars in that direction. What I saw actually caused me to gasp. I could see it very clearly. This monstrous creature stood at least seven feet and had black hair all over. It was walking on two very strong legs that looked human. The body was like that of a racing dog—in other words it had a very large chest and a small waist and hips. The arms and hands were huge and bigger than a powerful man [**sic**]. I couldn't see the fingers because it was carrying vegetation. The head was huge and covered in thick hair, but the face had an odd looking form. It was hard to make out since it was moving away from me but the jawline did extend out from the rest of the face... This wasn't a Bigfoot in my mind.[9]

After that, although an ardent hiker, Irving found himself "very wary of the wilderness." He described the event to "a couple of wildlife experts who probably thought I was crazy," though "one did say that there had been a 'wolfman' reported in the area back in the 1870s."[10]

Another anonymous blogger, writing in July 2011, recounted an event his father experienced as a teenager. On a snowy November night, year and location undisclosed, the blogger's father woke and went to get a glass of water in the kitchen. Peering through a window there, he saw "a dog/wolf like animal that looked to be six to seven feet long," standing in the middle of an old tractor road.

It heard him in the house and when it looked at him he could see its canine teeth well past its gum line. It had bright red eyes and walked on top of the snow. He yelled for his father who grabbed a single shot 16-gauge shotgun. My grandfather slid the window up and tried to fire but the gun's firing pin broke and would not discharge. This animal, they both to this day say, GLARED at them for what they think was about 30 seconds it let out a very loud growl and they said they could tell it was just plain evil. It then turned and walked back up the tractor road and went back into the woods.[11] ■

MAD DOGS & MONSTER HUNTERS

FERAL DOGS MAY BE RESPONSIBLE for some reports of canine cryptids prowling West Virginia. No reliable statistics exist for stray pets living wild in America, though some estimates for cats alone run as high as 70 million.[12] The feral dog census may be even higher: police in Detroit place the number roaming their bankrupt city around 50,000.[13]

All living creatures must eat, and strays are no exception, feeding when and where they can. In 1999, a survey by the US National Agricultural Statistics Service blamed feral dogs, at least in part, for the loss of cows, sheep, and goats valued at $37 million. Feral packs, if pressed, may also turn on humans, as they did with a ten-year-old St. Louis, Missouri, boy in 2001. "They were feeding off this kid," Police Chief Ron Henderson told the *St. Louis Post Dispatch*. I've seen over 1,500 bodies but I've never, never seen anything like this. Nobody has."[14]

A similar—though thankfully nonfatal—case occurred in West Virginia's Logan County, on May 30, 2011. Victim Emma Jude was walking on Millcreek Mountain, near the unincorporated community of Lake, when a pack of twelve or more dogs attacked from the darkness, mauling her severely. George Underwood, chief of Lake's volunteer fire department, learned of the attack from neighbors and transported Jude to Charleston's CAMC General Hospital, where her wounds were described as serious, but not life threatening.[15]

Though frequently described in media reports as "wild dogs," ferals should not be confused with true wild canids such as jackals, Australia's dingoes, and Africa's Cape hunting dogs. None of the latter species are domestic animals gone "wild" after abandonment by humans.

Coincidentally or otherwise, within a year of the attack on Emma Jude, rumors of "devil dogs" began to circulate through Logan County. Some accounts claimed that the canid prowlers targeted coyotes, disemboweling them and dining on their livers. Others say the coyotes were found drained of blood, vampire-style, but otherwise intact. Some locals scoffed at the reports, dismissing them as urban legends or an outright hoax.

Enter the Appalachian Investigators of

Credit: US Fish & Wildlife Service

PACKS OF FERAL DOGS CAUSE UNTOLD DAMAGE IN AMERICA AND AROUND THE WORLD.

AN ADVERTISEMENT FOR THE MOUNTAIN MONSTERS "DEVIL DOG" EPISODE ON DESTINATION AMERICA.

Mysterious Sightings (AIMS), a group of portly, bearded hunters led by John "Trapper" Price, stars of the *Mountain Monsters* "reality" series on Destination America. The show's six-episode first season premiered on June 22, 2013, visiting Logan County for an episode aired on July 6th. According to the promo for that episode:

There is a new apex predator in Logan County, West Virginia, wreaking havoc on the coyote population, the former top of the food chain. While local trappers are perplexed, AIMS has its own theory and suspects the legendary Devil Dog is to blame, sucking the blood and life from the coyotes. From eyewitness videos and pictures, the danger becomes even more apparent when they realize there is not one, but a pack of Devil Dogs on the loose and looking for blood. Something must stop this predatory pack before humans become their next target.[16]

With that in mind, the hillbilly huntsmen build a trap that snares two clearly feral dogs, while larger three-toed tracks allegedly are found around the site, suggesting that an aberrant "alpha devil dog" may have attempted to free its cohorts.[17] No dogs known to science are three-toed: all possess four toes on each paw, though some species also display vestigial dewclaws on their front or back legs. A three-toed carnivore of any species would be headline news in scientific circles, but *Mountain Monsters* spares its viewers anything resembling expert analysis.

AIMS returned for a second season in 2014 and tackled the "Werewolf of Webster County" on April 25, digging a pit in an effort to capture the beast. It may surprise no one to learn that the effort proved fruitless—as did my own search for tales resembling a werewolf encounter from Webster County. In Mason County, on the far side of the state, however...

■

>> "LIKE A WEREWOLF, ONLY SCARIER"

INEVITABLY, "DOGMAN" SIGHTINGS HAVE INSPIRED HOLLYWOOD HORROR FILMS.

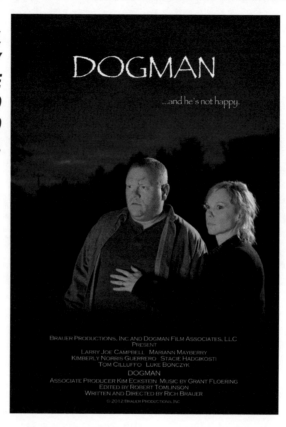

POINT PLEASANT, at the confluence of the Ohio and Kanawha Rivers, seems to be a haunted place. In Chapter 1 we examined a local "black panther" report, and Chapter 4 reviews the city's history of terrifying things with wings. More recently, on January 12, 2014, an unidentified resident reportedly saw a frightening creature near her Madison Avenue home, clearly visible beneath streetlights at 11:30 p.m. E-mail reporter Robbie Shaw describes the incident.

As she was having a smoke, she noticed movement, thinking it was someone walking down the railroad tracks. She looked

up and saw something that "blew her mind." It was, in her words, a thing that had a head of a dog, almost exactly like a German Shepard, and was walking like a person on two legs. She said she saw its eyes, and that's when she noticed it was staring at her. She said that she "became lost in its eyes." Any other description, she cannot recall clearly after seeing it look at her and then her seeing its eyes. She did tell me that it was either dark colored and almost had the look of wearing an oversized black sweatshirt (as in meaning it was rather large/bulky in the upper body), but she didn't think it was a sweatshirt, but *hair or fur. I asked her to clarify this. She said that's really the only thing she noticed and can remember, other than the head and description. She said the height was in the neighborhood of six feet, maybe just a bit less. She stated several times how the eyes "drew her in." She said the creature took a couple steps towards her, and at that time she saw a flash of light. The creature looked towards the direction it was originally heading and in a very quick movement, spinned [**sic**] and took off the direction it came from. The brief flash of light, she soon found out, was her mother's headlights as she turned into the road.[19]*

The witness told Shaw that the creature looked "like a werewolf, only scarier." Her mother, approaching the house, saw nothing. Shaw refers to an unidentified "government installation, located directly across from the witness's home," which "has an array of cameras installed over the entire property," speculating that it's "almost certain that this creature was recorded on their cameras."[20] Regrettably, no such facility appeared on any available map of Point Pleasant, or on Google Earth, as this book went to press. ∎

CHAPTER 4

"KEEP WATCHING THE SKIES!"

Those words of warning are the final line from Christian Nyby's 1951 sci-fi classic *The Thing from Another World*. As we shall see, they might apply as well to residents of West Virginia, where strange and terrifying creatures soar above treetops and towns.

THE GOLDEN EAGLE IS ONE OF WEST VIRGINIA'S LARGEST RECOGNIZED BIRD SPECIES.

BALD EAGLES RIVAL GOLDEN EAGLES FOR MAXIMUM RECORDS IN SIZE.

Credit: US Fish & Wildlife Service

A SNOWY OWL, CAUGHT IN THE ACT OF KILLING A DUCK.

Credit: US Fish & Wildlife Service

More than 300 species of birds may be found in the Mountain State during various seasons, though only seventy-five species officially live and breed year-round within its borders. The largest avian species, in order of size, are the golden eagle (*Aquila chrysaetos*), with a record body length of forty inches and a wingspan up to seven feet eight inches; the bald eagle (*Haliaeetus leucocephalus*), matching the golden eagle for maximum size; the black vulture (*Coragyps atratus*), with a record wingspan of five feet six inches; the great horned owl (*Bubo virginianus*), with a five-foot record wingspan; and the snowy owl (*B. scandiacus*), boasting a record wingspan of four feet eight inches.[1]

Aside from the carrion-eating vulture, all are efficient predators. None threaten humans, unless foolish individuals attempt to raid a brooding raptor's nest, but tales persist of West Virginia harboring much larger birds whose diet may include two-legged prey. Native Americans labeled those flying killers "thunderbirds," carving their hook-beaked images on totem poles, but are they merely beasts of legend? ■

ROC AROUND THE CLOCK

OUR FIRST REPORT of thunderbird depredation comes from the *St. Louis Globe-Dispatch*, published on February 24, 1895, under the headline "A Modern Roc." That heading referred to a giant bird of prey from Middle Eastern mythology, large enough to carry full-grown elephants. One such monster threatened Sinbad the Sailor in the Arabian Nights, and was graced with two heads by stop-motion animator Ray Harryhausen in his film *The Seventh Voyage of Sinbad* (1958).

West Virginia's roc, we're told, was smaller but still deadly. On February 1, 1895, it snatched ten-year-old Landy Junkins from her home at Bergoo (Webster County) and carried her off to parts unknown. On February 7, deputy sheriff Rube Nihiser and his son allegedly saw the monster attacking a doe and her fawn near the base of Owl Head Mountain, ripping the fawn away from its dying mother as Rube fired a useless rifle shot.

One day later, the bird attacked Peter Swadley, "a noted bear hunter of Webster" (Taylor County), leaving him badly wounded,

Credit: Author's collection

DEPICTION OF THE MYTHICAL ROC BY ARTIST CHARLES MAURICE DETMOLD (1883-1908).

with his clothes in shreds. Speaking in backwoods dialect, Swadley reportedly said, "Ef it was to come as ter how I should have ter pick atwixt a painter [panther] and the varmint, in fair hand-to-hand fight, I should take the painter every time."[2]

In retrospect, farmer Hanse Hardrick blamed the bird for stealing one of his sheep from its crude barn on Rattlesnake Run, eleven miles north of Addison (now Webster Springs, in Webster County), first tearing a hole in the roof. That raid, he said, had occurred sometime during the week between February 1st and 7th. Later sightings occurred around Snaggle Tooth Knob on Owl Head Mountain, where old-timer "Pap" Hammen recalled a pair of giant raptors roosting "many years ago."[3]

Compelling evidence of a huge flying cryptid at large? Cryptozoologist Mark Hall took the story at face value, as did author Patty Williams in her popular book *Haunted West Virginia* (2007). Researcher Chad Arment, however, takes a very different view, dismissing the tale as "nothing more than a newspaper hoax." The *Globe-Dispatch*, he writes, regularly "published articles on strange wonders of nature and technology as pure entertainment." To prove his claim, Arment conducted extensive research through microfilmed records of old West Virginia newspapers— including *The Call*, published in Addison—and found no mention of a giant bird at large in 1895, much less a monster snatching sheep and children.[4] There, for all intents and purposes, the matter rests.

Or does it?

One year after the roc spread its wings over Owl Head Mountain, another oversized raptor reportedly landed near Ranger, in Lincoln County. That story read:

> Hunting deer near the mouth of Vanatters Creek, Elias Midkoff and W. W. Adkins saw a very large bird circling high in the sky. As they watched, it rapidly descended and landed in the water. Adkins fired on it, crippling its wing, and waded into the creek to capture it alive. It fought him so furiously, however, that he was forced to kill it. It took five bullets to end its life.

A Baltimore newspaper, based on a description provided by Midkoff, stated, "The bird is seven, feet four inches from tip to tip, four feet from tip of bill to tip of tail, flat bill four inches long and eight inches wide, somewhat similar to that of a duck; web feet, neck nineteen inches long, and about 1½ inches through below the feathers; plumage dark brown, relieved on the wings and breast by light-blue shading.

Midkoff had traveled to Charleston to urge the State Historical and Antiquarian Society to dispatch a taxidermist to Hamlin in order to preserve the body of the mysterious bird. Apparently nothing came of the request.[5]

And nothing remains of the bird, presumably, if it existed at all. Clearly, from the description of its bill and feet, it was no raptor. Ducks belong to the family Anatidae, with geese and swans. The largest species known to visit West Virginia seasonally is the trumpeter swan (*Cygnus buccinator*), with a record body length of six feet and a top wingspan of ten feet two inches, but its snow-white plumage bears no resemblance to the bird at Vanatters Creek. No native duck matches the specimen described, in either size or coloration.

Flap forward to August 1978, when another large bird visited Oceana (Wyoming County). Witness Edward Cook reported three sightings of the creature near his home, on Clear Fork Road. "He lit three days in a row right up there," Cook said, pointing from his front porch to a nearby ridge. The bird's plumage was "a silver-blue color. Its wingspread is something enormous. Maybe that wind storm earlier this summer forced it down."[6]

Perhaps, or maybe there was something else at work, since Oceana also had a second cryptic visitor that month: a tall, dark night-prowler in quasi-human form, able to leap great distances from standing starts (see Chapter 9). Cook saw the latter thing, as well, agreeing with policemen who pursued it that it "was no bird."[7]

Our next report of giant birds at large in West Virginia was posted to the Internet in July 2004. The anonymous blogger refers to witnesses Abe and Mildred Patterson, traveling with their children on US Route 19 along the New River, to visit relatives in Fayetteville. It was a "fine August day," the year undisclosed. Spying a picnic table at roadside, the Pattersons stopped for lunch and were still unpacking the car when young daughter Emily screamed in terror. Abe and Mildred, with son John, rushed to find the girl battling with "an incredibly large crow." The blogger writes, "She was trying to run and so kept getting further and further into the brush, away from anyone who could help her. By the time her father caught up with her she'd lost both her eyes. Two weeks later, she died of a strange infection."[8]

Fact or fantasy? The tale sounds outlandish, and indeed seems to be fiction. My personal inquiries in Fayette County, including the local newspaper and public library, revealed nothing to suggest the incident ever occurred.

Stan Gordon, a longtime paranormal researcher and author based in Pennsylvania, logged our next report. The event allegedly occurred near Clendenin, in late September or early October of 2007, as an unidentified motorist followed a two-lane road in broad daylight, around 8 a.m. Rounding a curve, the driver slammed on his brakes to avoid striking a large, winged creature standing on the pavement, eating roadkill. As described to Gordon, the bird-thing stood at least four feet tall, with a "dominant" head poised above the car's roofline. Its head was bare above a long and "somewhat crooked" neck, separated from the bird's coat of thick dark feathers by "a very dominant yellowish orange collar of plumage." Its chest was "very distinct and well formed," while the dark body perched atop bare feet and legs.[9]

"We both startled each other it seems," the driver remarked, "for it looked as shocked as I was. In seeing me, it turned from me and in an awkward way, ran from my vehicle so as to fly away. It was more like a jumping, hopping run which took probably a distance of five yards before its absolutely huge wingspan lifted it into flight. Its wingspan easily was as wide as the two lane road which we were on." The driver later measured the road's width, a total of twenty-one feet.[10] He told Gordon:

The wings were, as I can remember, as arms of a human are attached. It had shoulders. It had a very muscular upper torso and the wings were as if they were its arms. The wing beat, as you put it, seemed distinct, not panicky or cumbersome but distinct in its fluid motion. The only thing cumbersome was the gait in which it seemingly ran jumping from one foot to the other in a hopping manner while flapping to gain speed to take off. As the bird did gain flight and in flapping away, it appeared the wings were massive feathered arms. Shoulders were evident, however not huge athletic sized shoulders.[11]

After his sighting, the witness did some research in an effort to determine what he'd seen. Gordon writes, "He said the closest thing that he could find, was a drawing of a teratorn, an extinct bird."[12]

In fact, the family Teratornithidae includes at least five species of prehistoric birds, with a sixth species disputed. The largest, *Argentavis magnificens*, known from fossils found in Argentina, boasted a wingspan of twenty feet or more, tipping the scales at 176 pounds, and is presumed to be extinct for some eight million years. The next largest species, *Aiolornis*

A RECONSTRUCTION OF THE PREHISTORIC TERATORN, A "THUNDERBIRD" CANDIDATE.

incredibilis, known from fossil finds in California and Nevada, believed extinct for at least 11,700 years, had an eighteen-foot wingspan. *Teratornis woodburnensis*, known from fossils found in California and Oregon, also presumed extinct for some 11,000 years, had a fourteen-foot wingspan. *Teratornis merriami*, with more than 100 specimens retrieved from California's La Brea Tar Pits, presumed extinct for 10,000 years, was a relative pygmy: its wingspan was only twelve feet six inches. The fifth confirmed species, *Cathartornis gracilis*, is known only from a few leg bones unearthed in California, making estimates of its overall size problematic.[13]

"Teratorn," from the Greek *Teratornis*, translates as "monster bird"—an accurate description of these ancient predators, at least in terms of size. But are they still clinging to life in modern times? Cryptozoologists Ken Gerhard and Mark Hall, among others, suggest that possibility, while doubters scoff, subjecting them to ridicule. ■

>> THE FLATWOODS MONSTER

OUR NEXT REPORT REMOVES US from the realm of flying predators and leads us into Ufology, for West Virginia's most famous case of a "monster" at large. More than sixty years after the fact, the case remains controversial, acceptance or denial posing a litmus test for believers and skeptics.

The tale began in Flatwoods (Braxton County), at 7:15 p.m. on September 12, 1952. Brothers Eddie and Freddie May were playing football with friends Tommy Hyer, Gene Lemon, Neil Nunley, and Ronnie Shaver, assisted by Lemon's dog, when they saw a fiery object blaze across the sky, apparently falling to earth on a nearby farm owned by G. Bailey Fisher. The boys ran to fetch Kathleen May—mother of Eddie and Freddie—who grabbed a flashlight and joined them on their trek to the crash site. After a quarter-mile hike, they crested a hill to discover a pulsating "ball of fire" surrounded by mist that made their eyes and noses sting. Amidst the fumes, Gene Lemon saw two smaller lights beneath a tree, and Mrs. May turned her flashlight in that direction, receiving a shocking surprise.

Before them stood a nightmarish ten-foot-tall creature, generally humanoid in form, wearing a garment resembling a dark, pleated skirt. Its head was heart-shaped, or perhaps it wore a heart-shaped cowl; the witnesses could not decide. Its face was red and glowing from within, with bulging eyes, while its torso was green. Short arms, ending in long, claw-like fingers, protruded as if sprouting from its chest. Pinned by the flashlight's beam, the thing emitted a shrill hiss and moved toward the intruders, then veered off toward the fireball while they fled in terror.

Safe at home once more, Kathleen May phoned Sheriff Robert Carr, then called A. Lee Stewart Jr., co-owner of the *Braxton Democrat*. Both men interviewed the witnesses, then Stewart returned to the Bailey farm with Gene Lemon, reporting that "there was a sickening, burnt, metallic odor still prevailing" on the hilltop. Sheriff Carr and Deputy Burnell Long, searching separately, professed to find nothing.[14]

The next morning, Stewart returned to the site and found two elongated tracks in mud, with traces of an unidentified "odd, gummy deposit." These, he wrote, might indicate a "flying saucer" landing, since the area had seen no automobile traffic for several years.

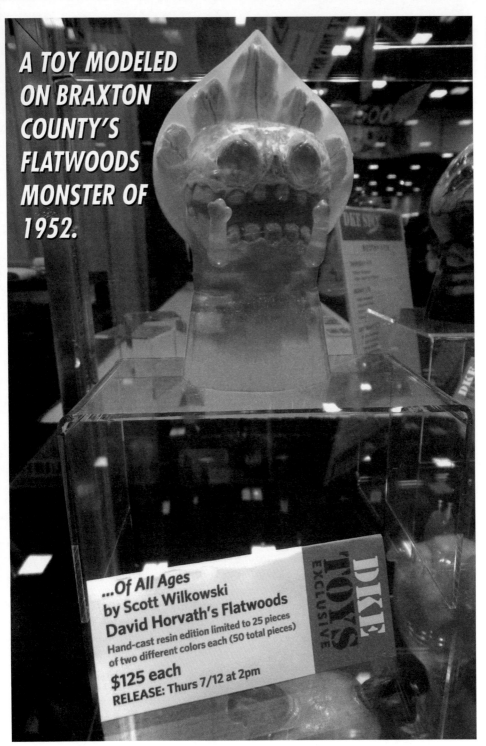

A TOY MODELED ON BRAXTON COUNTY'S FLATWOODS MONSTER OF 1952.

...Of All Ages
by Scott Wilkowski
David Horvath's Flatwoods
Hand-cast resin edition limited to 25 pieces
of two different colors each (50 total pieces)
$125 each
RELEASE: Thurs 7/12 at 2pm

DKE TOYS EXCLUSIVE

Credit: US Fish & Wildlife Service

SOME SKEPTICS PROPOSE THAT THE FLATWOODS MONSTER WAS A COMMON BARN OWL.

That theory crumbled when a local man, Max Lockard, admitted driving his ten-year-old pickup to look for the monster, a few hours prior to Stewart's second visit.[15]

Next on the scene were William and Donna Smith, representing a group called Civilian Saucer Investigation. Circulating around Flatwoods, the Smiths found several other witnesses who claimed similar sightings. Two locals, a mother and her adult daughter, reported seeing the Flatwoods Monster a week prior to September 12, confirming its appearance and eye-watering stench. The daughter was so traumatized, her mother said, that she had spent the next three weeks at Clarksburg Hospital. Gene Lemon spent the night after his incident convulsed and

vomiting, left with a sore throat that lingered for several weeks, and other members of the search party reported lesser symptoms, mainly inflammation of the throat and sinuses.

Explanations for the Flatwoods incident are predictably diverse and contradictory. On September 23, the *Charleston Gazette* dismissed the UFO as a falling meteor, and the monster as an illusion created by the "meteor's gas."[16] No meteor was found on Bailey Fisher's farm, but that would not stop skeptics from assuming its existence for the next half century.

Author Donald Keyhoe, writing in 1953, asserted that two plainclothes agents from US Air Force Intelligence visited Flatwoods after the monster sighting, posing as magazine writers, and decided that the UFO had been a meteor that "merely appeared to be landing when it disappeared over the hill."[17] Which, if true, scuttles the *Gazette*'s claim that "meteor gas" from a crash created some monstrous illusion.

Author Ivan Sanderson took another view entirely, asserting that "a flight of aerial machines" was "maneuvering in formation" over Braxton County when one fell to earth "and its 'pilot' or 'occupant' managed to get out before it disintegrated. He or 'it' did so in a space suit or the equivalent of our deep-sea-diving bells, regulated to counteract gravity by adjustment to the density of air at ground level."[18]

According to Donald Keyhoe, his unnamed Air Force investigators concluded that the ten-foot-tall, red-and-green creature described by seven witnesses was, in fact, "a large owl perched on a limb," with underbrush beneath it lending "the impression of a giant figure." Frightened witnesses then had "imagined the rest." Professional skeptic Joe Nickell narrows the focus to one owl species in particular: *Tyto alba*, the barn owl, which boasts a record body length of 19.7 inches and a top wingspan of three feet, seven inches. Barn owls are neither red nor green, but such discrepancies mean nothing in the search for what debunkers label "truth."[19]

In March 2010, the History Channel's *MonsterQuest* series branded the Flatwoods creature a "lizard monster," deploying "the latest high-tech search gear to uncover this mysterious beast that has terrorized this town for almost sixty years."[20] The search proved futile since, in fact, the thing had not been seen by anyone since 1952. That does not mean the monster is forgotten, though. Each year, in Flatwoods, residents stage a three-day festival including live music, visits to the Fisher farm, and tours of the "Green Monster" museum. ■

SUGAR CREEK

THE FLATWOODS FUROR has eclipsed another incident—or series of incidents—occurring elsewhere on the same night. New Yorkers George and Edith Snitowsky were traveling between Frametown and Gassaway when their car died near Sugar Creek. Moments later, they noticed a nauseating odor and George went to track it down. Professor James Gay Jones of Glenville State College describes what happened next.

Crossing over a slight rise to the left of the highway, he saw, some sixty yards down the slope, a large spheroid moving slowly back and forth as it hovered over the ground and from it came a soft, violet light. On moving closer to the object, he felt the sensation of thousands of needle-like vibrations irritating the skin of his whole body. Nauseated, he turned and stumbled back toward the car.[21]

Edith screamed as George returned, warning of something behind him. Turning, he saw "a figure about eight or nine feet tall with a big head, bloated body, and long, spindly arms gliding rapidly toward him," barely thirty feet distant. Racing to the car, George slid inside and locked the doors, cowering with Edith below the dashboard while one long, inhuman arm "forked at the end" slid across their windshield. Soon, frustrated, the creature floated away. After a trembling eternity, the Snitowskys saw its spheroid craft rise above the treetops and soar off into space. With its departure, their engine came to life and George drove on to the nearest gas station, where he found a V-shaped burn mark on the auto's hood.[22]

As if those doings were not strange enough, author Frank Feschino Jr. claims the incidents at Flatwoods and Sugar Creek were only parts of a bizarre UFO cascade over West Virginia on September 12, 1952. Speaking in August 2008, Feschino claimed that three alien spacecraft landed repeatedly in the Mountain State that night, hop-scotching across the landscape before they finally departed.

"There were ten actual crash landings that night in West Virginia," Feschino told Beckley's *Register-Herald*. "They're all documented. This is what took seventeen years to figure out." Other touchdowns supposedly occurred at Oglebay Park near Wheeling; at Holly, Frametown and St. Albans; three around Charleston; and five along Cabin Creek in Kanawha County. "I actually re-drove and re-enacted that whole night, driving all through Braxton County," Feschino said. "It took me years to do it. It was a cold case and I reconstructed it."[23]

Skeptics remain unimpressed. ■

>> MOTHMAN

A NEWSPAPER ARTICLE COVERING MOTHMAN'S FIRST APPEARANCE AT THE "TNT AREA."

THE MOUNTAIN STATE'S NEXT MONSTER scare developed gradually. In autumn 1965, a child told his mother he had seen "an angel...a man with wings" outside their home, near Clendenin, but she laughed it off. Months later, during summer 1966, a doctor's wife living on the Ohio River saw a six-foot "giant butterfly" swoop past her, but fearing ridicule, she told only a handful of her closest friends. On November 1, 1966, a National Guardsman saw "a large, brown, man-shaped figure" perched in a tree near the armory on Point Pleasant's Camp Conley Road.[24]

The first "official" sighting of the creature later known as Mothman occurred on November 12, 1966, while Kenneth Duncan and four friends were digging a grave for his brother-in-law at a small cemetery in Reamer, near Clendenin. Duncan told reporters the creature looked like "a brown human being. It was gliding through the trees and was in sight for about a minute," though his four companions failed to glimpse it.[25]

Three days later, on the night of November 15, two married couples—Steve and Mary Mallette, with Roger and Linda Scarberry—went for a drive in the "TNT Area," an old munitions dump seven miles north of Point Pleasant, dotted with concrete domes locals called igloos. It was a common trysting spot in those pre-Mothman days, but on this night romance took a backseat to terror. Approaching the site, both couples saw an eerie figure slouched at roadside, watching them with "two big red eyes, like automobile reflectors." "It was shaped like a man, but bigger," Roger said. "Maybe six and a half or seven feet tall. And it had big wings folded against its back. For a minute we could only stare at it. Then it just turned and sort of shuffled back towards the open door of the old power plant. We didn't wait around."[26]

Escape proved difficult, however. As they sped back toward Point Pleasant on State Route 62, Linda saw the thing following them, now airborne on wings at least ten feet across.

"I could hear it making a sound," Mary declared. "It squeaked like a big mouse." And it kept pace with the fleeing car, even when the speedometer's needle hit 100 miles per hour. "It followed us right to the city limits," Roger said. "Funny thing, we noticed a dead dog by the side of the road there, but when we came back a few minutes later, the dog was gone."[27]

A midnight snack, perhaps.

A sheriff's deputy accompanied the frightened couples on their second trip to the TNT area. This time they saw nothing, but the deputy's two-way radio began emitting weird sounds "like a speeded-up phonograph record," until he switched it off.[28]

Publication of the couples' story brought forward another witness, contractor Newell Partridge, residing in Doddridge County, 100 miles northeast of Point Pleasant. On the night of November 14th, Partridge said, his television "began acting like a generator" and his German Shepherd "started carrying on something terrible." Stepping outside with a flashlight, Partridge swept the beam across a nearby field and saw something with eyes like "red reflectors" on a bicycle. His dog charged the figure and vanished in darkness, never to return.[29]

Mason County Sheriff George Johnson held a courthouse press conference on November 16th, reporting that four more locals had seen a similar creature around Point Pleasant in recent days. While not discounting their statements, Johnson opined that the thing was a "freak shitepoke"—a nineteenth-century slang term for herons.[30] (The nickname derives from a heron's tendency to defecate when flushed from cover.) Five heron species may be found in West Virginia— the largest being the great blue heron (*Ardea herodias*), with a record standing height of four feet six inches and a maximum wingspan of six feet seven inches—but none is capable of speeds approaching 100 miles per hour.

The same was true when Dr. Robert L. Smith, a wildlife biologist at West Virginia University, suggested that Mothman might be a sandhill crane (*Grus canadensis*) straying from its usual migration route.[31] Gray overall, with a red forehead, sandhill cranes commonly stand three feet ten inches tall, with a record wingspan of six feet, ten inches, but their top speed cannot rival Mothman's.

Despite disclaimers from Sheriff Johnson and Dr. Smith, sightings of Mothman continued—at least twenty reported encounters, involving forty-seven identified witnesses, between November 16, 1966, and November 2, 1967. Four times, the creature crossed into Ohio, including one appearance at Lowell, on November 26, 1966, where multiple witnesses saw "four giant brown and gray birds with red heads," each roughly five feet tall, with ten-foot wingspans. Point Pleasant was ground zero for the West Virginia sightings, though Mothman strayed as far as Campbells Creek and St. Albans. Six of the state's sixteen sightings emerged from the TNT Area, though searches of the property failed to reveal Mothman's lair.[32]

Folklorist Jan Harold Brunvand inflates the total of Mothman encounters, claiming that "at least 100 people saw the monster, and perhaps twice as many were afraid to report their sightings." Finally, he concedes, "Something real may have triggered the Mothman scares, but the stories—whatever their sources—also incorporated existing folklore."[33]

Six weeks after the last reported Mothman sighting, a disaster shocked Point Pleasant. On December 15, 1967, the Silver Bridge— linking Point Pleasant to Gallipolis, Ohio— collapsed during rush hour, claiming forty-six lives, including two victims whose bodies were never recovered. Investigators blamed the collapse on a defective eyebar in one of its suspension chains, combined with poor maintenance and daily loads far exceeding

A BUNKER IN POINT PLEASANT'S "TNT AREA."

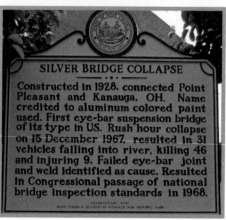

Credit: Author's collection

A MEMORIAL FOR VICTIMS OF THE SILVER BRIDGE COLLAPSE IN DECEMBER 1967.

Pleasant and the TNT Area through 1968, many reported in the Athens, Ohio, *Messenger* by local correspondent Mary Hyre. Gradually, encouraged by authors such as John Keel and Gray Barker, some grieving residents began to view Mothman as a harbinger of doom— or perhaps an instrument of disaster. That theme continued with release of *The Mothman Prophecies,* a horror film based on Keel's book of the same title, in 2002.

Author Loren Coleman has compiled a "Mothman Death List," with eighty-four purported victims at last count, in August 2005. Beginning with the Silver Bridge unfortunates, Coleman proceeds to list "deaths linked to the original series of Mothman sightings of 1966-1967, to the release of the

the bridge's design tolerance. It was a tragedy, but not the first bridge failure in America, nor would it be the last.

Those other sites, of course, had not been visited by Mothman. It took some time for locals to connect their flying phantom with the Silver Bridge collapse, but UFO and "monster" sightings continued around Point

YEARS AFTER THE EVENTS, MOTHMAN REPORTS INSPIRED A POPULAR HORROR FILM.

RICHARD GERE · LAURA LINNEY

THE

MOTHMAN

PROPHECIES

BASED ON TRUE EVENTS

movie in January 2002, to the various cable premieres, and VHS/DVD releases later in 2002 and 2003."[34] Included are original witnesses, reporters and investigators on the scene—Mary Hyer, Ivan Sanderson, Fred Freed, Gray Barker, D. Scott Rogo, John Keel—and *Mothman Prophecies* director Ted Demme. Other inclusions are a stretch, such as fourteen-year-old Aaron Rebsamen, who died unexpectedly at his Arkansas home in May 2003. Aaron's father, renowned crypto-artist William Rebsamen, painted the cover for Coleman's book *Mothman and Other Curious Encounters,* but neither he nor his son had any personal connection to the case.

Debunker Joe Nickell briefly tackled Mothman in 2004, writing vaguely that "[a] popular legend of the Point Pleasant area holds that 'Mothman' was the creation of a prankster" in costume, but he quickly abandons that thesis, admitting that several glory hounds had claimed to be the one and only joker. Nickell finally concludes that Mothman sightings "were mostly caused by owls— probably more than one type."[35]

Nickell's first vote goes to the barred owl (*Strix varia*), based on its "strong" eyeshine, with a secondary nod to the larger great horned owl. The former species has a record body length of twenty-five inches, with a top wingspan of four feet one inch. The latter,

"medium" eyeshine notwithstanding, is significantly larger and commonly adopts a defensive posture resembling some sketches of Mothman.

Ironically, author Mark Hall—mocked by Nickell, who brands him a "cryptozoologist" with sarcastic quotation marks included[36]— also suggests that Mothman may have been an owl. Not just any owl, however, but an undiscovered giant species Hall dubs "Bighoot," previously known to Native American tribes as the predatory "Flying Head." Hall suggests a giant, unknown species of eagle-own (genus *Bubo*), but also mentions *Ornimegalonyx*, the Cuban Giant Owl, that stood three feet six inches tall. Unlike Mothman, however, small wings restricted *Ornimegalonyx* to flying only short distances.[37] A truly giant owl, if one exists, would make a better Mothman candidate than any species recognized by modern science.

Fortean author Jerome Clark, writing in 2000, reported continuing Mothman sightings in West Virginia. Early witness Linda Scarberry told Clark that she and husband Roger had seen the creature "hundreds of times, sometimes at close range." "It seems like it doesn't want to hurt you," she remarked. "It just wants to communicate with you."[38]

These days, Mothman communicates primarily with tourists in Point Pleasant. Sculptor Bob Roach unveiled his twelve-foot-tall metallic statue of Mothman in 2002, at the city's first Annual Mothman Festival, presently a two-day event held on the third weekend of September.

Three years later, Jeff Wamsley opened the Mothman Museum and Research Center. As at Scotland's Loch Ness and elsewhere, money flows in. "It's helped the town," says Ruth

A FANCIFUL STATUE OF "MOTHMAN" IN POINT PLEASANT, WEST VIRGINIA.

THE GREAT HORNED OWL IN A PROSPECTIVE "MOTHMAN" POSE.

Finley, co-owner of the 106-year-old Lowe Hotel on Main Street. "People come because of Mothman and they stay at the hotel, they go to the restaurants." Jack Fowler, director of the more conventional Point Pleasant River Museum, resents the creature's legacy. "With all the history we have here," he remarked in 2008, "what do people come here for? That darn Mothman."[39] ■

> BIRDMEN

MOTHMAN, AS IT TURNS OUT, did not land in Mason County altogether unannounced. Appalachian folklorist James Gay Jones tells us:

> In the early 1900s at Point Pleasant, a large bird with the head of a man and a wingspan of at least twelve feet was seen. It appeared just prior to or immediately after the oc-

currence of a tragic event. By World War I a birdman was observed flying over Looneyville, up Johnson Creek, down Gabe in Roane County thence down Elk Valley into the Kanawha. Its monstrous size and dark reddish feathers which glistened in the sunlight cast fear in all who saw it. Parents kept their children indoors after sightings. After World War II people said they were chased by a huge bird while traveling on the highways of Mason, Jackson, and Wood Counties near the Ohio River.[40]

That flying monstrosity, or its twin, reappeared on State Route 2, at Mason County's Chief Cornstalk Wildlife Management Area, in 1960 or '61, frightening a motorist and her elderly father near the Ohio River. The anonymous driver explained:

I slowed down, and as we got closer we could see that it was much larger than a man. A big gray figure. It stood in the middle of the road. Then a pair of wings unfolded from its back and they practically filled the whole road. It almost looked like a small airplane. Then it took off straight up...disappearing out of sight in seconds. We were both terrified. I stepped on the gas and got out of there. We talked it over and decided not to tell anybody about it. Who would believe us anyway? [41]

Another common owl?

In 1968 and '69, John Keel reports that UFOs swarmed the Point Pleasant region, accompanied by "tall hairy creatures with luminous eyes," and that "a winged giant was also seen on a few rare occasions." Mary Hyre investigated those sightings for *The Messenger*, but Keel writes that she "published very few of them."[42] Sadly, no further details have survived her passing. ■

>> SEA MEETS SKY

FORTEAN BLOGGER LON STRICKLER has published multiple reports of yet another flying cryptid in the Mountain State, this one distinctly fishy, rather than bird- or manlike. The first incident occurred between 6 and 7 p.m. on December 3, 2004, as an artist riding with a friend along Route 2, toward a Huntington art show, spied a bizarre airborne creature. As told by Strickler:

I noticed a sudden movement in the sky over the Ohio River to my right in front of the car. It was a grayish, smooth, winged shape. The shape swooped in a figure eight right in front of the windshield and then was suddenly gone to the left of us. It didn't fly out of sight; it was just gone. This happened very quickly, but as I am a visual artist, it was impressed into my memory banks![43]

Nor was the creature difficult to see. It was "bigger than the car," with a wingspan "wider than the two-lane road we were on. The wings seemed to stretch wider somehow as it did the figure eight swoop. It was never more than twenty-five feet away from us as it flew towards the windshield." The witness saw "only body and wings—no head, eyes, tail, or feet. It did not look humanoid in any way. On the other hand, it wasn't a bird either. It moved more like something in the ocean would move—did not flap the wings like a bird, or flutter them like a bat, but stretched them instead."[44]

The thing was gray, like Mothman, but "translucent like a jellyfish. As it banked and swooped I could see many angles of it and somehow it looked more transparent as it turned some parts to us. I immediately thought it was like a manta ray."[45]

Strickler reports a second sighting of a similar cryptid, emailed to him by another unnamed correspondent during August 2010. This time, the location is omitted by a male witness who "encountered a huge ray-shaped thing straddling the road ahead of him. Initially, it was visible only as two reddish-orange spots that he mistook for bicycle reflectors in the fog. When he honked his horn, the 'reflectors' blinked at him, then the whole body lifted up off the road and sort of glided down over the hill to disappear into the fog-filled valley below."[46]

Other sightings, perhaps related, include a driver's report of a "manta-shaped something" circling over his car near Horton (Randolph County), and a child's report of a white "furry" thing, four feet wide, with no apparent head or limbs, flying beside the family car at some undisclosed location. At Wheeling, near the Foggy Bottom Family Fun Center, a similar creature allegedly snatched a resident's dog.[47]

I feel safe in saying that manta rays (genus *Manta*) have not abandoned the sea and learned to fly while breathing air, or developed a taste for dogs in lieu of shrimp and plankton. Neither are they found—at least, officially—in mid-Atlantic waters matching West Virginia's latitude. Their farthest penetration to the north, on record, has been the coastline of South Carolina. Clearly, something else is flapping through the Appalachian skies, if we can trust reporting witnesses, and it bears no resemblance to any species of bird known to science. ■

CHAPTER 5

SHEEP-SQUATCH

What is white and wooly, the size of a bear, with a doglike head, sprouting horns like a goat's, and jutting tusks, paws resembling the "hands" of an oversized raccoon, a long pointed tail, and an acrid stench of sulfur? The answer: Sheepsquatch, also known in West Virginia as "The White Thing," feared by those who've seen it and by thousands more who know the beast only by reputation.

MODEL OF MYLODON IN CHILE'S CUEVA DEL MILODÓN NATURAL MONUMENT, WHERE FOSSILS WERE FOUND IN 1896.

Credit: Author's collection

MEGALONYX, A GIANT GROUND SLOTH PRESUMED EXTINCT FOR 11,000 YEARS, HAS BEEN PROPOSED AS A POSSIBLE SHEEPSQUATCH CANDIDATE.

"Sheepsquatch" takes its name in part from Sasquatch, also known as Bigfoot, that elusive hairy ape-thing seen by witnesses the length and breadth of North America, and for its seeming coat of wool, ranging in hue from dirty yellow to a pristine white. Reported from at least eight counties in the Mountain State, it ranges from the Northern Panhandle southward, appearing with particular frequency along the Ohio River, on Mothman's turf.

Mary Hyre collected stories of "man-bears" prowling on Jericho Road, in Point Pleasant, but failed to publish them before her death at age fifty-four, in February 1970.[1] Three anonymous reports, posted online long after the fact, also refer to sightings spanning decades, but without specific dates.

E-mail correspondent "Carrie," writing in July 2004, claimed that Sheepsquatch "screams like a woman and has been known to hurt people. This creature will mostly warn you when there is going to be a death, but sometimes I think it gets angry with people!" Her great-uncle Sam was allegedly one of its victims, stalked and mauled while walking through a wooded hollow in the dark of night, left with deep cuts on his back. Sam described his assailant as "a white furry bear with a man's face and feet, with a woman's scream," standing seven feet tall.[2]

A FERAL HOG, SUGGESTED BY SOME AS A POSSIBLE SHEEPSQUATCH CANDIDATE.

Another Internet poster, also writing in July 2004, recalls hearing tales of The White Thing "since I was very young." One such story came from his/her grandmother, who met the creature in Mingo County one snowy night, while walking in search of aid for an ailing baby. As told online, "She described this anomaly as being white in color, looking similar to a cow, but sitting much too low to the ground to be one. She did not, however, feel threatened in any way. Her impression of the presence was that it was protecting and guiding her through the storm. At all times, it kept its distance from her and her sick infant."[3]

Word of that encounter spread swiftly, prompting a local man to relate his own tale of bizarre events occurring several days earlier. According to the second witness, Sheepsquatch had dragged him from his home and up a nearby mountainside. "Once there," the blogger wrote, "the creature had spoken to him and shown him bright colorful lights leading up to the heavens. The creature had told him that he was to tell none of their encounter or he would die."[4]

No other case on record has Sheepsquatch engaged in conversation, but the tale is offered here without comment.

Yet another anonymous correspondent, writing in August 2011, reports hearing tales of The White Thing in Ragland (Mingo County) "for a very long time...Several trusted friends of mine have told of their encounters with the thing." One friend "said it could run faster than anything he'd ever seen in his life and that it stood up on two legs like a man and was tall." Two others met the creature while riding ATVs, first sold in the mid-1960s. While riding beside railroad tracks, they saw "a thing run across their path on four legs like a dog, then jump on a stack of railroad ties that are 4½ feet tall on two legs before leaping an excess of ten feet to the hillside." The writer concludes, "All I could link them possibly to is the reported satanic worship that was said to have taken place in the bottom, up the road from 24 Hollow, which is right beside a battery shop in Ragland."[5]

Once the Devil shows his face, logic goes out the window—but there was little logic to start with, regarding Sheepsquatch.

A spate of sightings in the 1990s brought The White Thing back to public consciousness.

In 1994, witness "Mike P." had his first encounter with Sheepsquatch near a friend's home in New Cumberland (Hancock County). The boys were playing in a camper, parked in the yard, when they saw "something that looked like a large, white bear...[I]t stood up on its hind legs and was about six and a half feet tall. It turned and ran through the woods away from us, breaking sticks and medium-sized limbs off of trees as it went."[6] Other reports of that event online misplace it in Boone County, while describing it identically.[7]

A second encounter from 1994 involves Ed Rollins, a US Navy veteran raised in Gallipolis, Ohio, who was fascinated by reports of Mothman just across the river. After leaving the service, he visited Mason County to investigate that mystery, "My logic being that if I tried, seriously and diligently, to disprove the stories, and failed, then I would have strengthened their credibility." To that end, he prowled the woods and hollows surrounding the TNT Area, questioned surviving Mothman witnesses, and pursued tips from "an acquaintance at a UFO investigation group who I considered a marginal flake."[8]

And in the process, he collided with another mystery.

While exploring the woods along Bethel Church Road, Rollins heard "something large" crash through the undergrowth ahead.

Believing it to be a dog or stray cow, he was shocked to meet "a large, brownish-white creature: its fur looked dirty and matted as if the animal did very little in the line of self grooming...The creature moved on all fours as it breached the brush line and knelt to drink from the creek.

Its front limbs, the only limbs I saw clearly, ended in what were markedly paw like 'hands.' Its head was long and pointed, like a canine's, and it had largish horns: not antlers but single point horns." Concealing himself, Rollins watched the thing drink from a creek, then amble off without sighting him, leaving a strong smell of sulfur behind.[9]

In retrospect, Rollins could not decide if he had seen "a dirty white animal or a brownish animal with a white undercoat." He dismissed supernatural causes for the beast's sulfuric odor, blaming pollution of the TNT Area from manufacture of gunpowder and other explosives whose chemicals contaminated the soil and water supply.[10]

In 1995, a couple driving through Boone County saw a large grayish-white animal crouched in a roadside ditch. It resembled a bear in form and general size, but the witnesses claimed that it had four eyes. They stopped to get a closer look, whereupon the thing charged their car. They fled, and on arriving home discovered scratches on the fender of their vehicle. One explanation offered for the thing's four eyes is that the couple, in their fright, mistook small horns for eye sockets.[11]

Four years passed before the next reported Sheepsquatch sighting, this one again involving witness "Mike P." He was back with his friend in New Cumberland, camped outside town, when both boys heard movement in the woods at 2 a.m. They emerged from their tent to investigate, and "all of the sudden, the White Beast appeared out of the darkness and charged at us. We jumped up and ran back to his house; all the while this thing was chasing us. The thing stopped at the wood line and let out a terrible scream. Then it just turned around and headed back into the woods. The next morning, we examined the trail, and the ground was so torn up that it appeared as though someone had taken a tiller all the way out the trail."[12] Once again, other reports of the same incident online misplace it in Boone County.[13]

Our first report from the twenty-first century was posted online by witness "Tess" in July 2004, but occurred "a few years ago." Driving from Huntington to Charleston, Tess and her two companions decided for reasons unstated to detour fifty miles out of their way and pass through Point Pleasant. Heavy snow overtook them near Arbuckle, slowing their progress to five or ten miles per hour, though Tess maintains that she "had good visibility." Rounding a curve, she says,

I looked to my left, and about a foot from my window I saw what appeared to be a strange creature, half man, half animal. It had a face very similar to a sheep, horns like a ram, and it was standing upright like a human. I was so stunned, and immediately thought I had lost my mind! My friends started screaming, "What in the hell was that?"

So I backed up the car, and it looked at me, turned and ran into the woods. I got a pretty good look at it. It basically had its nose right in my face! It was white, furry, and had paws, no hooves, paws like a dog, a sheep-like face, and stood upright like a human. It ran away on human legs... Needless to say we discussed this all the way home, and could not come up with any animal we know that resembled it. No, I had not been drinking, and up until this point had control of all my facilities [sic].[14]

Another report posted online in July 2004 comes from witness Brett Hutchinson,

describing events from mid-January. While hiking through woods near Four States (Marion County), Hutchinson heard "something rustling in the brush about 100 yards away" and went to investigate, later writing, "I wish I'd stayed home." Cresting a rise, he saw "what appeared to be a large white bear walking along the ridgeline." After several moments, the beast saw Hutchinson and ducked into the woods. "I've had friends tell me I'm crazy," he wrote. "Others tell me it was just an albino bear, but I know better. It was like nothing I had ever seen in my life."[15]

Amy Sharp posted a Sheepsquatch report online in July 2004. While riding with her boyfriend near Pumpkintown (Randolph County) around 8 p.m., they saw another car parked at the side of the road and slowed to look for signs of a possible accident.

Then we saw this thing moving down in the ditch. We pulled the car to the side of the road to see what it was. This thing looked like it had four eyes. Then, all of a sudden, it jumps out of the ditch and starts attacking the car. I have no clue what the thing was, but it was bigger than a dog, a lot bigger. I told my boyfriend to go back to see what it was, but he wouldn't...Now, every time I ride down back roads, I always watch the woods to see if I can see that thing again...and I always keep my doors locked, too.[16]

Parallels with the 1995 report from Boone County are inescapable. Was that account a third party's garbling of Amy Smart's encounter, or did Smart lift details from the earlier report to perpetrate a hoax online? If so, why change the location and omit the supporting detail of damage to her boyfriend's car? It is another nagging Sheepsquatch mystery, defying resolution.

Witness "Melissa" posted yet another report online during July 2004. She was traveling toward Winfield (Putnam County) with her husband, at night on Route 35, when she "looked ahead and saw something. About fifty yards ahead of us was something in the road. It was on all fours and was snow white. It was bigger than a dog, way bigger. As we got closer it turned and looked our way. Its mouth opened and it stood up on two legs and began running across the road and up through the woods." Husband Joe asked if Melissa had seen the creature, but she was speechless and burst into tears. Deciding to go home, they detoured through Poca, refusing to go back the way they had come.[17]

Witness April Clitis waited two years to report her meeting with Sheepsquatch in 2009. While walking with a friend through Glen Rogers (Wyoming County), around midnight, Clitis thought she heard someone following them. At first, she tried to ignore the sounds, blaming kids or "some creepy guy," but it finally got on her nerves and she pulled a flashlight, directing its beam backward along their path. She writes:

As I turned my flashlight on I saw this tiny kitten and as it was crossing the road about twenty feet ahead it went from being this tiny kitten to this mountain lion like thing

only different. It was laying down almost so close to the ground that I couldn't really tell what it was. All of a sudden I shined my light directly on it and saw it stand up and stare at me with these green eyes. It had legs that bent inward like a jumping cat. I really to this day can't explain what it was or how it was possible, but I remember it looking straight at me, smiling kinda with these teeth bared, and then jumping over into the trees.[18]

Clitis saw the same thing, or its twin, near the same spot in Glen Rogers on a subsequent evening.

The second time I saw it I was with my boyfriend, in the car. We were arguing, and all of a sudden I looked up and there it was standing in the trees next to the car, staring at me and him. I started the car, turned it around, and drove down the road. When I hit the same curve where I saw it before, this deer jumped out and scared the Hell out of me. My boyfriend laughed at me, but that thing scares the crap out of me every time I think about it.[19] ∎

>> UNUSUAL SUSPECTS

IF SHEEPSQUATCH EXISTS, WHAT IS IT?

We may safely rule out polar bears (*Ursus maritimus*), which, while large and white, are never naturally found outside the Arctic Circle. Other white bears do exist, including a blond variant form of black bears (*U. americanus*), the Kermode "spirit bears" of British Columbia's Great Bear Rain Forest, where they are protected by law. An albino grizzly bear (*U. arctos horribilis*) has also been seen and photographed in the same Canadian preserve. Montana game wardens captured an albino black bear at Glacier National Park in October 2009, transporting it to a safer, more remote location beyond reach of hunters.

The arguments against Sheepsquatch being a white bear are fourfold. First, no bears known to science have horns. Second, none possess paws resembling raccoon "hands." Third, no bears sport long pointed tails. Finally, while bears can certainly stand, walk, and even "dance" on their hind legs, none travel in that way for any significant distance, and none are capable of running like a man on two legs alone.

Another suspect suggested by skeptics is the feral hog (*Sus scrofa*). Feral hogs are the ancestors of domestic pigs, fully capable of interbreeding with their tame cousins since Spanish explorers introduced them to the New World in the fifteenth century. Today, they roam by the millions across thirty-nine states, including West Virginia, pillaging crops and native flora, devouring smaller animals, and spreading diseases including pseudorabies, swine brucellosis, classical swine fever, African swine fever, bovine tuberculosis, influenza, blue-ear pig disease, anthrax, tularemia, West Nile virus, salmonella, trichinosis, streptococcus, and *Escherichia coli*. Hunting in West Virginia, and elsewhere, has thus far failed to curb the invaders' ever-growing population.

Wild boars have tusks, like the fangs sometimes seen on Sheepsquatch, and they may reach impressive sizes. "Hogzilla," shot in Georgia on June 17, 2004, reportedly measured twelve feet long and weighed more than 1,000 pounds. When scientists examined its remains in March 2005, they scaled its weight back to 800 pounds, with a length somewhere between six feet ten inches and eight feet six inches—still an impressive porker.[20]

Another specimen, dubbed "Pigzilla," was allegedly shot in Alabama on May 3, 2007. Its eleven-year-old slayer posed for an astounding photograph, with his gun behind the porcine giant's corpse. According to the hunter and his parents, Pigzilla measured nine feet, four inches and tipped the groaning scale at 1,051 pounds. Media investigators panned the photo as a posed shot doctored to exaggerate scale, depicting a farm-raised pig known in life as Fred, purchased by the young killer's father four days before it was shot. A grand jury convened to investigate charges of animal cruelty in 2008, but adjourned without filing indictments.[21]

So, we have tusks on feral hogs, and albino specimens have been photographed. In the negative column: no horns, no "hands" (all pigs have cloven hooves), and absolutely no ability to walk—much less run—on two legs.

Another proposed Sheepsquatch suspect is *Megalonyx* ("great claw" in Greek), a genus of the sloth family Megalonychidae, presumed extinct for some 11,000 years. Living two-toed sloths (genus *Choloepus*) belong to the same family, inhabiting rainforests of Central and South America. *Megalonyx* was much larger than its extant relatives, eight to ten feet long, with its top weight estimated at 2,200 pounds. Fossil remains of the type specimen, *M. jeffersonii*, measured about nine feet nine inches long.

That specimen is significant to our study of Sheepsquatch because US Vice President (later President) Thomas Jefferson proposed the generic name *Megalonyx* in 1797, describing the remains—found in western Virginia—in a paper titled "Certain Bones," presented to the American Philosophical Society. French zoologist Anselme Gaëtan Desmarest appended Jefferson's surname as the sloth's specific epithet in 1822, but American naturalist Richard Harlan gets formal credit for naming the genus *Megalonyx* three years later.[22]

In its heyday, *Megalonyx* roamed throughout North and Central America, ranging as far north as the Yukon. It lived from the Hemphillian of the Late Miocene (10.3 million years ago) to the Rancholabrean of the Pleistocene (11,000 years ago), when Paleo-Indian hunters hounded the sloths to extinction. In 1804, President Jefferson asked explorers Meriwether Lewis and William Clark to watch for living *Megalonyx* specimens on their long trek from St. Louis to the Pacific Northwest, but none were observed. Today, *Megalonyx* is the official state fossil of West Virginia.

But are any of the ancient creatures, or some variant evolved since their presumed extinction, still alive? It seems improbable, and there are still The White Thing's horns to be explained. And yet...

Another giant prehistoric sloth— *Megatherium* ("great beast" in Greek)—has been proposed as a candidate for a South American cryptid called *Mapinguari* or *Isnashi*, said to roam the jungles of Brazil and Bolivia. Its native names translate as "roaring animal" and "fetid beast," respectively, the latter attesting to its foul odor. Descriptions of the *Mapinguari* are even more bizarre than those of Sheepsquatch: some witnesses describe a single Cyclopean eye, long claws, armored skin like a caiman's, backwards-pointing feet, and a second mouth on the creature stomach. The hide deflects arrows, spears, and even bullets. In fact, the creature's only weakness is a fear of water, causing it to shy away from lakes and rivers.

Like Sheepsquatch, the *Mapinguari* displays a fierce, erratic temperament. There are no stories of it guarding mothers and their infants, but on the ferocious side, one report from 1937 describes a *Mapinguari's* three-week

rampage in Brazil, leaving 100 cattle slain, their tongues ripped out.

While some witnesses describe the *Mapinguari* as a bipedal primate in the mold of Bigfoot, others sketch a slothlike creature. *Megatherium* appears to fit that mold, from its long claws to the bony dermal ossicles embedded in its skin like armored plates. In life, between the Late Pliocene (3.6 million years ago) and its presumed extinction 10,000 years ago, *Megatherium* was the largest ground sloth, the size of modern elephants at twenty feet in length and weighing up to 8,000 pounds. Only mammoths and the hornless rhinoceros *Paraceratherium* were larger.

A smaller ground sloth, *Mylodon,* also survived in South America until roughly 10,000 years ago. Considerably smaller than *Megatherium,* at ten feet tall on its hind legs and 440 pounds, *Mylodon* shared its larger relative's long claws and hide pebbled with dermal ossicles. Neither genus walked on backwards-pointing feet to baffle predators, nor did they eat through stomach-mouths. Sloths are primarily herbivorous—or, more properly folivorous, preferring leaves—but some modern species supplement their diets with insects. None are carnivorous, and while a giant sloth could certainly kill cattle with its seven-inch claws, more delicate operations, such as extracting tongues, do not seem feasible. ■

A.I.M.S. TO THE RESCUE

PERHAPS IT WAS INEVITABLE. On May 9, 2014, during their second season on Destination America, the hairy Appalachian Investigators of Mysterious Sightings tackled The White Thing on their *Mountain Monsters* series. As advertised in advance: "The team fights against the terrifying Sheepsquatch and his potent urine."[23] After some zany driving, wood-knocking, claw marks on trees, blurred thermal footage, and a dose of alleged Sheepsquatch urine that briefly blinded Trapper John, the team went home empty-handed. ∎

CHAPTER 6

ALL WET

West Virginia is a relatively "dry" state, with only 0.6 percent of its total land mass underwater. By comparison, 41.5 percent of Michigan is submerged, 15.7 percent of New Jersey, 15 percent of Louisiana, and 4.7 percent of California. Where, we might ask, are aquatic cryptids to hide?

SOUTH AMERICAN PIRANHAS HAVE REPORTEDLY BEEN CAUGHT IN WEST VIRGINIA RIVERS.

The Mountain State is landlocked, so we have no tales of sea monsters plying its nonexistent coastline. More surprisingly, it has only one natural lake, Hardy County's two-acre Trout Pond. West Virginia's other 213 lakes and ponds are all manmade, the ten largest created by impoundment dams built and operated by the US Army Corps of Engineers. Stonewall Jackson Lake ranks as the largest, sprawling over 2,790 acres, with an average depth of fifteen feet and a maximum depth of eighty-two feet.[1] The state's deepest body of water is Summersville Lake, at 327 feet. Only two other lakes—Tygart and Bluestone—claim depths exceeding forty feet.[2]

Manmade lakes pose two major problems for would-be monster hunters. First, as we have seen, most are relatively shallow. Second, all are relatively new lakes—in West Virginia's case, constructed during the twentieth century. Logically, none should harbor any unfamiliar species, and certainly no "living fossils" left over from prehistoric times, as is sometimes suggested for famous "monster" lakes such as Scotland's Loch Ness and Vermont's Lake Champlain.

Nonetheless, we do have two reports of lake monsters in West Virginia, both presented on the Internet's Global Lake Monster Database. For what they may be worth, they read:

> On March 12, 2002, someone said that while visiting a lake in West Virginia he saw a[n] eight foot long "shape" moving just under the surface of the water, about fifty-five feet away. When closer, it was revealed that it had "four flippers, a very short tail, [and] a long neck with what seemed to be a very narrow head." In a lake a few miles away, a "plesiosaur-like beast 10-11 feet long...ambushed a deer from shallow water." If anyone knows more info about this please send me the info via e-mail.[3]

That site was last updated in 2006, with the plea for further information still unanswered. Barring revelation of more details—or at least the names of the two lakes—we must pronounce those cases closed and look elsewhere for unidentified swimming objects.

■

>> RIVERS RUN THROUGH IT

IF WEST VIRGINIA is short on lakes, the same cannot be said of rivers. Statewide, the DNR counts 8,289 rivers, streams, branches, creeks, drains, forks, licks, and runs supporting aquatic life forms, plus five swamps large enough to rate names. Scientists recognize 179 fish species in West Virginia, of which 154 are native to the state, with the remainder being accidental or intentional introductions.[4]

Discovery of new freshwater fish species is rare in the United States, but one such find was reported from West Virginia in February of 2008. That species is the diamond darter (*Crystallaria cincotta*), a translucent fish apparently restricted to the lower Elk River, whose adults range from three to five inches in length. Stuart Welsh, an assistant professor in the Wildlife and Fisheries Resources

THE DIAMOND DARTER, A NEW SPECIES OF FISH DISCOVERED IN WEST VIRGINIA IN 2008.

Credit: US Fish & Wildlife Service

Program at the Davis College of Agriculture, Forestry and Consumer Sciences, named the diamond darter. "The discovery of a new species in West Virginia is not something that happens every day," he told reporters. "If there is one fun and exciting thing about science, then it is the discovery of new things. Discovering and describing a new species is directly linked to discovering the diversity of life."[5]

And so, we might add, is cryptozoology. ∎

UNWANTED

DNR AGENTS WORRY more about invasive fish species than new discoveries. Thus far, they claim that West Virginia's waters are free of voracious snakeheads (family *Channidae*), though specimens have been caught in neighboring Maryland and Virginia. Asian carp (family *Cyprinidae*) are well established in the state, weighing up to 100 pounds, devouring native species and endangering boaters with their erratic leaps from the water.[6]

One family of invaders seldom mentioned by the DNR—never officially acknowledged as inhabiting the Mountain State—is the Characidae: piranhas and the closely related pacus, both native to South America. Piranhas, of course, are globally notorious for their ferocity in pursuit of fresh meat. Pacus, while closely resembling piranhas, lack their sharp teeth and are omnivorous, prompting some collectors to call them "vegetarian piranhas."

BEAUTY AND THE BEAST: A POSTER FOR PIRANHACONDA.

Aliff's father placed the twelve-inch fish in a live well and phoned a DNR biologist. "He told us it might be a piranha," Eugene Aliff said. "Later we showed it to a guy who had spent a lot of time in a pet shop, and he confirmed it as a piranha."[8]

DNR Chief of Fisheries Bret Preston urged the public to stay calm, telling McCoy, "It probably came from someone who had it in an aquarium and turned it loose in the river, probably fairly recently. I doubt if it would have survived the kind of wintertime water temperatures we get around here." While avoiding further details, Preston added, "It happens from time to time, when a piranha gets too big for an aquarium and its owner decides to turn it loose. We've had piranhas show up in the Ohio and Kanawha rivers."[9]

In December 2010, e-mail correspondent Jessica Woods posted another piranha story online, this one from Chapmanville, in Logan County. She wrote:

> *My boyfriend went fishing a lot this summer...He caught some good sized fish like drums, catfish, carp, bass, but never a bluegill or sunfish. He caught a fish that we weren't sure of at the time, but now we know what it was. We froze it in the freezer, going to use it for catfish bait later on. I saw the same fish as he caught on a TV show. It was a silver-colored piranha fish. I am positive of this 100% and I know fishermen stories of how things get bigger of a tale every time that they are told, but this is not one of them I assure you...I've never seen anything like this ever, and I'm sure it wasn't a gar fish. 100% piranha fish![10]*

Pacus pose no danger whatsoever to humans or their livestock. Piranhas, on the other hand, are viewed with great alarm when they are found swimming at large in the United States. Pulp fiction and Hollywood horror films have inflated their killer reputation to the point of hysteria, lapsing into slapstick comedy with features such as *Mega Piranha* (2010) and *Piranhaconda* (2012, cross-bred with a giant snake).

Ten-year-old Hunter Aliff hooked a much smaller, but no less startling, specimen on August 19, 2007, while fishing with his father and an adult friend at Lower Falls, on the Coal River near St. Albans. After a struggle, he reeled in his catch, mistaking it for a large bluegill (*Lepomis macrochirus*) until it bit through his line while thrashing around on the riverbank. "As soon as my finger touched its jaw, I could tell how sharp its teeth were and I pulled back," Aliff told reporter John McCoy of the *Charleston Gazette*. "I'd have to say that this is the most unusual thing I've ever caught."[7]

Regrettably, the post included no photos or contact information for the author, and must therefore be regarded as unverified. ∎

> OGUA

WEST VIRGINIA'S FIRST REPORTS of aquatic cryptids date from the mid-eighteenth century, when European settlements were established in the region of present-day Marion County, along the Ohio River. Native tribesmen knew the amphibious beast as Ogua, described as a monstrous turtle, larger than a bear, sometimes two-headed, hiding in the Ohio and Monongahela by day, emerging to hunt after nightfall.

Aboriginal tradition has it that sixteenth-century Mohawk chief Hiawatha dreamed the Ogua into existence as a means of driving white trespassers from his territory, but since European settlers did not reach the future West Virginia region for another century, modern historians trace the legend's birth to local Delaware or Shawnee tribes instead.[11] In any case, the monster clearly failed to do its job.

The first report of a white man's encounter with Ogua dates from October 1746. Two pioneer families, named Nichols and Taylor, had built adjoining cabins beside the Monongahela River a year earlier, intending to farm the district. On October 22, while fishing in the river, a twelve-year-old son of the Nichols clan was dragged underwater by something his companions described as larger than a bear, with a turtle's body. Searchers turned out in vain, but the following day, the boy's father found a large curved bone wedged between two trees, assuming it belonged to one of the amphibious predators. Days later, a Nichols daughter woke to the sound of something rubbing against the outer wall of her family's cabin. Peering through a crack between two logs, she glimpsed a large, shaggy beast "bigger than a sow." Both families soon abandoned their homesteads.[12]

A second account of Ogua was recorded four decades later, in a letter archived at West Virginia University's Regional History Center in Morgantown. The author was a young soldier assigned to Fort Harmar, built in 1785 near the site of present-day Marietta, Ohio, at the Muskingum River's confluence with the Ohio. He wrote to his parents:

There is an animal in this country which excites the imagination of all who have had the opportunity to view it; being amphibious, it resides in the water during the daytime, but at night repairs to the land in quest of its prey; which are deer. They lie in the deer paths undiscovered, behind an old stump, until the deer, unaware of its enemy, passes over him; this creature immediately seizes him, and entangling him in its tail, which is fifteen feet in length, and notwithstanding all the deer's exertions to free himself, draws him to the water, where he drowns and devours him.

Some of our men lately discovered one of the formidable creatures early in the morning with its prey, of which they informed some of the company who were nigh; they soon came up with him and killed the giant beast with clubs. The monster weighed 440 pounds.

They lurk in deep underwater caves with no bottom and their head resembles a giant turtle [sic]. Woe to any man who chances upon one of these formidable predators unarmed. The Indians call them Oguas.[13]

Nearly two centuries later, on May 15, 1983, Marion County's *Fairmont Times* reported that local fishermen "have been troubled of late by something that seems to be a sea monster, or possibly just a plain river monster." According to the newspaper:

The monster...is said to be at least twenty feet long. The thing is described as being reddish brown in color, it has a serpent-like head with a mouth lined with razor-sharp teeth and a long flat tail that churns the water into foam, as it turns around after standing the fisherman's hair on end.[14]

Recent witness George Cochran, a local jeweler, saw Ogua while boating on the Monongahela, admitting that "he did not get a very good look at it and it did not trouble him."[15] Later that summer, Fairmont coal miner John Edward White left his work on the night shift early, thanks to a broken ventilation fan. Hoping to catch some fish for breakfast, he stopped on Route 19 and took his pole beneath a bridge spanning the river, near the mouth of Paw Paw Creek at Rivesville. Moments later, White saw many small fish breaking water, as if fleeing from a larger predator. David Cain described what happened next, in an article for the monthly magazine *Wonderful West Virginia.*

Suddenly a huge fin exploded six to eight feet straight up out of the murky depths about thirty feet from him! Startled, John instinctively leaped back from the river's edge. A large serpentine tail rose out of the water and, with a powerful sweep, the unknown creature turned and dived into the dark depths.[16]

No other source describes Ogua as having fins. The tallest dorsal fins on record, up to six feet high, are found not on fish, but on a mammal—the orca or killer whale (*Orcinus orca*)—whose presence in a West Virginia river would truly be astounding.

Cain's article was illustrated with a picture captioned "A creature photographed where people claim to have sighted Ogua."[17] In fact, as anyone can see, the "creature" has been drawn—and rather clumsily, at that—over a stock photo of water. Its pose is virtually identical to one of many photos faked by late hoaxer Frank Searle, allegedly depicting the Loch Ness Monster.[18] ∎

>> HORROR ON THE OHIO

ON JULY 8, 1893, the *Pittsburgh Post* carried the following report from Wood County, West Virginia.

A few weeks ago dispatches from below [Parkersburg] stated that a sea serpent was alarming people down the Ohio River. Boating parties here during the past week have been greatly frightened by the appearance of the monster with a head as big as a barrel. The freak has been vari- *ously described as eight to fifteen feet long, appearing to be floating on the surface of the river, often near Negle's Island. When approached the monster would dive with great commotion of the waters, making heavy waves that were dangerous to open boats.*

Last night a party of a dozen prominent young people, who are entirely reliable, were out on a large boat when the monster suddenly appeared, crossing the river in front of them. They were panic stricken and made frantic efforts to get away from the locality without making an investigation. Parties living along the river state that the monster can be seen daily, showing most conspicuously when heading up the river, and apparently changing the abode frequently. All descriptions of the strange monster agree, and the truth of the story is not doubted in this locality.[19]

The story spread, reaching as far as Winnipeg, Manitoba, by mid-September, but no further substantive details emerged.[20] At least one portion of the original story is incorrect: there is no "Negle's Island" in the neighborhood of Parkersburg. The author likely meant to say Neal Island, a sandbar directly offshore from Vienna (Wood County), now part of the Ohio River Islands National Wildlife Refuge. Whatever the creature was—if it existed at all—labeling it a "sea serpent" was clearly erroneous. The Ohio River flows between Pittsburgh and Cairo, Illinois, having no contact with the sea.

In passing, we should note that Parkersburg lies just ten miles to the southwest of Marietta, Ohio, near the site where soldiers allegedly killed an *Ogua* in the late eighteenth century.
■

THE HOULT RIVER, ALLEGED HOME TO AN AQUATIC CRYPTID KNOWN AS "OGUA."

THE BLACKWATER RIVER, SCENE OF AN OCTOPUS CAPTURE IN MAY 1946.

>> SUCKERED

IF ORCAS HAVE NO BUSINESS in West Virginia's rivers, neither do cephalopods. The molluscan class Cephalopoda ("head-feet" in Greek) consists of two distantly related, extant subclasses: Coleoidea, including octopuses, squids, and cuttlefish; and Nautiloidea, represented by *Nautilus* and *Allonautilus*. All have arms or tentacles lined with suckers extending from their heads and squirt ink when alarmed. All known species live exclusively in salt water.

It was a surprise, therefore, when fishermen Ross Saunders and Robert Trice pulled a three-foot-long octopus from the Kanawha River near Charleston, on December 24, 1933. Afterward, speaking to the *Charleston Gazette*, Saunders and Tice claimed the creature had attacked their skiff, wrapping its arms around the bow, whereupon Tice "plunged a knife in its gullet and hauled it aboard with his crutch." According to the newspaper, "Two theories of the unusual fish's presence in the Kanawha river centers [*sic*] around the possibility that it made its way from the Gulf of Mexico by

AN OCTOPUS PULLED FROM THE BLACKWATER RIVER IN 1946.

way of the Mississippi and Ohio rivers or it may have been lost from an aquarium aboard a boat."[21]

In fact, neither turned out to be the case. On December 29 the *Gazette* announced that the whole incident was a hoax. City detectives E. N. Shuck and John Wooster said they were seeking Ross Saunders and an unnamed accomplice, wanted on suspicion of stealing a barrel of fish shipped from Boston to a local grocery store. The shipment included an octopus, prized as a delicacy, which the unnamed thief allegedly gave to Robert Trice as his prop for "a swell Christmas joke."[22]

That prank was forgotten by January 10, 1946, when four boys in Thomas (Tucker County) arrived at school bearing two octopuses weighing twenty pounds apiece, pulled from the North Branch of the Blackwater River. One, they said, came from a miniature lake created by the Fairfax Electric Company power dam, where discharges from the plant's

turbines kept water warm year-round. The other had been found and shot some distance below the dam. The boys also had killed a third specimen, weighing about fifteen pounds, "but threw it back into the water thinking it was not an unusual catch."[23]

Principal Stelman Harper examined the two dead cephalopods, measured their thirty-inch tentacles, and phoned "fish experts" at Davis & Elkins College, hoping to solve the mystery, but they were clueless. Speaking to reporters, Harper "expressed doubt they could have been placed there by a returned veteran from the South Pacific," adding that "it would have been almost impossible for anyone to have shipped them into the community without arousing curiosity, due to their size."[24]

That mystery remains unsolved, as does the capture of another octopus in 1954, pulled from a creek near Grafton, twenty-eight miles northwest of Thomas. All we know about the latter incident, today, was stated in a snippet from the *Pittsburgh Press*.

An octopus in a creek near Grafton, W. Va. Found by four nameless boys who gave it to the dog-catcher, logically. "Two-foot long tentacles." It died shortly.[25]

The early hoax aside, Mark Hall suggests that West Virginia's recurring cephalopods of the postwar decade may have come from the Canaan Valley in northeastern Tucker County, an oval, bowl-shaped upland valley encompassing extensive wetlands and the headwaters of the Blackwater River, which exits the valley at Blackwater Falls. Once the bottom of a Pleistocene sea, Canaan Valley later sheltered species fleeing the advance of man: West Virginia's last wild elk were killed there by hunters, in 1843.[26] Noting that the

valley was unsettled until midway through the Civil War, Hall writes:

Such a place might have harbored some rare form of life such as these eight-legged creatures where they have gone unnoticed except for the occasional puzzling captures reported in 1946 and around 1954. My suggestion is that these creatures might be a unique form of freshwater cephalopods that find their way into the rivers of West Virginia from the Canaan Valley. If an investigation were to be made for such creatures it might best begin with an examination of that swamp.[27]

So far, alas, none has. ■

>> DEVIL'S HOLE

OUR FINAL AQUATIC CRYPTID is doubly shrouded in mystery, presented without dates, from an obscure location. West Virginia author William B. Price reported the incidents in 1963 and named their site as Devil's Hole, somewhere along the Cheat River, which flows from Hendricks (Tucker County) to join the Monongahela River at Point Marion, Pennsylvania. Today, no Devil's Hole is recognized along the Cheat's 78.3-mile length, but old-timers place it at the bottom of Cheat Lake, formerly Lake Lynn Reservoir, created by erection of Lake Lynn Dam in 1925. The lake's average depth is twenty feet, approaching ninety feet near the dam.

The stories told by Price are odd, to say the least. One incident involved a group of loggers transporting freshly cut timber downriver. Hiram Gillum tumbled from the raft at Devil's Hole, but caught one of its binding ropes to keep from sinking. Suddenly, a beast rose from below. It "seemed to have a half-human face, horns like a goat, and a great sucker-like mouth. Its claws, it seemed, were webbed for swimming." While Gillum kicked the thing with his spiked boots, a companion struck it with a pike and drove it back into the depths, permitting Gillum to reboard the raft.[28]

A second incident involved fishermen Jake Price and John Pyles, trolling the Cheat River for catfish and suckers when they reached Devil's Hole. As with Hiram Gillum before him, Price tumbled from his raft, alerting the monster below.

Then the creature appeared. Its black head had moss-covered horns and its eyes looked like hot coals. Its claws pulled Jake down by his shoulders. Its sucker-like mouth closed over his mouth. Instead of sucking the life out of Jake, the creature got his chaw of tobacco. He worked his way free and was saved. John Pyles then threw a harpoon into the creature causing a flow of blood. The creature was thought to have been killed.[29]

Whatever lived in Devil's Hole—if anything—no further sightings have been logged since the attack on Price. Eyewitness descriptions of the creature, while agreeing with each other, match no species known to science from the ancient past to modern times. It seems that both attacks occurred before the Lake Lynn Dam was built, defeating skeptics' arguments that these, like other "gill man" sightings, may have been inspired by 1950s horror movies, such as *Creature From the Black Lagoon* and *The Monster of Piedras Blancas*. The mystery endures. ■

THE DEPARTMENT OF NATURAL RESOURCES FOR WEST VIRGINIA STATES: "RECENT REPORTS FROM MARYLAND AND VIRGINIA ON THE PRESENCE OF SNAKEHEAD FISH IN THEIR WATERS ARE CAUSE FOR CONCERN FOR WEST VIRGINIA. SNAKEHEADS HAVE NOT BEEN COLLECTED BY OUR FISHERIES STAFF, OR REPORTED CAUGHT BY ANGLERS IN WEST VIRGINIA WATERS, BUT THEY HAVE BEEN FOUND IN A PET SHOP AND IN A HOME AQUARIUM."

CHAPTER 7

"THERE ONCE WERE GIANTS"

Worldwide, the mythology of every race and nation speaks of humans grown to monstrous size, whether as aberrant individuals or races of their own: the Hebrew Nephilim, Celtic Fomorians, Titans and Cyclopes of Greece, the Yaks of Thailand, Puntan of Micronesia, Nunhyunuwi of the Cherokee—the list is virtually endless. Nor were giants strictly relegated to the realm of legend. Rather, ancient historians regarded them as predecessors and contemporaries of all races recognized today. Greek poet Homer, writing in 400 B.C.E., declared without a hint of doubt, "On Earth there once were giants."

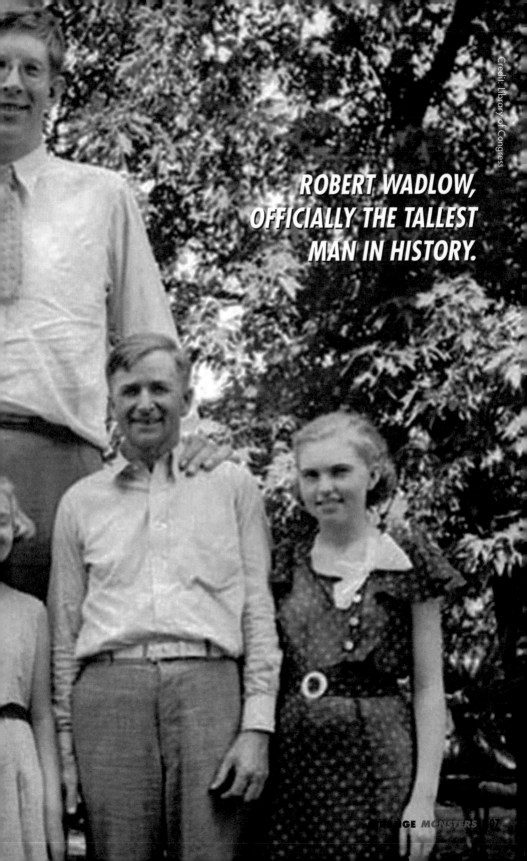

ROBERT WADLOW, OFFICIALLY THE TALLEST MAN IN HISTORY.

But were there giants, really?

The tallest person verified by Guinness World Records was American Robert Pershing Wadlow (1918-1940), who measured 8 feet 11.1 inches and weighed 440 pounds when he died, at age twenty-two. Today's record holder is Sultan Kösen of Turkey, measured by Guinness at eight feet three inches in February 2011. The tallest woman, China's Zeng Jinlian, measured 8 feet 1¾ inches at her death in 1982, but could not stand fully erect because of spinal curvature.

Such individuals, historically, have been dismissed as "freaks," their size attributed to over-production of growth hormone in childhood. But did whole races of giants exist? And if so, did their range extend by any chance to West Virginia?

The answer, it seems, is at least a qualified "yes." ■

>> GRAVE CREEK

WEST VIRGINIA'S GRAVE CREEK MOUND, SITE OF ENIGMATIC ANCIENT BURIALS.

Credit: Author's collection

MOUNDSVILLE (MARSHALL COUNTY) is named for its famous Grave Creek Mound, an earthen structure sixty-two feet high and 240 feet in diameter, ostensibly created by members of the pre-Columbian Adena culture, c. 250-150 B.C.E. Excavation of the mound by white settlers began in 1830, and eight years later, diggers reportedly found two "large" skeletons, male and female, the latter adorned with copper bracelets. Also found was the enigmatic Grave Creek Stone, a small sandstone disk said to bear "an inscription in unknown characters."[1] Unfortunately for proponents of "forbidden" archaeology, the same symbols are found in a book published in 1752, suggesting a possible fraud. The stone survives today, but no trace of the oversized couple remains. ■

MARION COUNTY

ANOTHER TANTALIZING STORY comes from old Palatine, now East Fairmont. There, sometime in the 1850s, workmen digging a root cellar allegedly unearthed two human skeletons measuring "more than seven feet tall." We are told that "many curious onlookers" viewed the remains before they "mysteriously disappeared overnight," presumably stolen for sale to some unknown collector. If so, they have not resurfaced in the past 160-odd years.[2] ■

MURDER IN WHEELING?

MORE SPECIFIC INFORMATION is available on West Virginia's next giant, published in *The Western Literary Messenger* of February 1857. That item—quoting from the *Wheeling Times*—reads:

Skeleton of a Giant Found—A day or two since, some workmen engaged in subsoiling the grounds of Sheriff Wickham, at his vineyard in East Wheeling, came across a human skeleton. Although much decayed, there was little difficulty in identifying it, by placing the bones, which could not have belonged to other than a human body, in their original position. The impression made by the skeleton in the earth, and the skeleton itself, were measured by the Sheriff and a brother in the craft locale, both of whom were prepared to swear that it was ten feet nine inches in length. Its jaws and teeth were almost as large as those of a horse. The bones are to be seen at the Sheriff's office.[3]

Renowned cryptozoologist Dr. Karl Shuker adds a strange footnote to that affair, writing: "It was soon dismissed as a hoax, however, when one of the newspapers announced that three bullets had been found in its skull."[4] Shuker notes that the "bullets" were not described further, and we are left to marvel at the fact of a murder victim nearly eleven feet tall—almost two feet taller than the largest human giant on record—so airily dismissed by authorities. As with other giant remains from West Virginia, the Wheeling skeleton has vanished. ■

>> RIVESVILLE

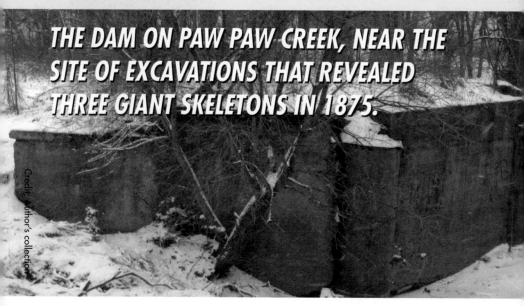

THE DAM ON PAW PAW CREEK, NEAR THE SITE OF EXCAVATIONS THAT REVEALED THREE GIANT SKELETONS IN 1875.

Credit: Author's collection

WORKMEN MADE ANOTHER startling find in 1875, while building a bridge at Rivesville, near the mouth of Paw Paw Creek. This time, there were three giant skeletons, with strands of reddish hair still dangling from their skulls. A local physician was summoned, and while "exposure to air deteriorated the bones rapidly,"

his "careful measurement" reportedly established that "the skeletons had supported people approximately eight feet tall."[5] We are left with an implication that the bones soon crumbled into dust, thus explaining their unavailability for further study. ∎

>> HORNY IN PRESTON COUNTY

OUR NEXT SET of ancient remains are not huge, but nonetheless rank as extremely peculiar. Their description, published in 1882, is worth presenting in full.

Sandy Creek Mound is the third and last in the county, and is situated on the old McGill farm, three miles east of Fellowsville, on a ridge between the forks of Little Sandy. It was fifteen feet high and twenty-five

feet across at the base, being circular in form, and was used as an internment mound. Its summit was crowned with a large ash tree. The Indians had buried in its top, and the Moundbuilders in its base.

That the Moundbuilders were cremationists is beyond doubt. This is established by the appearance of the bones, which everywhere show the action of fire, as well as by the ashes and charcoal found. Most probably they placed the corpses in a sitting posture, and piled wood around them and fired it. On the remains earth was thrown. The dead were placed in one at a time. When one of their people died, the mound was opened, the corpse was placed beside the one last put in, and the fiery process repeated. A careful examination of the bones show[s] no traces of death by violence, and seems to contradict the theory that all the dead in these mounds were slain in great battles.

From this mound, the writer obtained a strange skull out of the top layer of bones. Digging down, we came upon several skulls in the bottom layer, but could not get them out, as they crumbled to pieces in our hands; finally the top of one was secured, and where the sutures meet on the top of the Caucasian head, they were prevented in this head by a small bone of about one inch in length by one half inch in width, of a peculiar shape. All the other skulls possessed this same peculiar bone. The top of the skull secured and the others that crumbled, showed the heads of the race to have been long and narrow, with low foreheads, and long narrow faces.[6]

A tribe of normal size, then—but with slender heads and horns! ■

> SMITHTOWN

WHITE DAY CREEK, SITE OF ANOTHER GIANT DISCOVERY IN 1882.

WEST VIRGINIA'S NEXT REPORT of giant remains, found in September 1882, take us to Monongalia County. Amateur archaeologist F. M. Fetty and his wife were exploring Whiteday Creek, near Smithtown, when an unusual rock formation captured their attention. It masked a shallow cave, which they entered, discovering a "false wall" at the rear. Shifting several large stones, they reportedly found "the remains of a giant human in a sitting position with artifacts of stone and flint surrounding the prehistoric cadaver."[7]

At this point in our journey, we expect the bones and other relics to evaporate—and such, indeed, turns out to be the case, another disappointment for inquiring minds. The story has an epilogue of sorts, however, as we read of a second similar discovery nearby, in the summer of 1883.

Reports credit James A. Faulkner with finding the second giant skeleton near Smithtown. He summoned local doctor Samuel Kramer to examine it, resulting in a measurement of seven feet four inches. From that, Dr. Kramer "deduced the living person must have been almost eight feet tall."[8]

And there, as usual, the story ends, in mystery. ■

>> SPRING HILL & BEYOND

IN 1884, Professor Cyrus Thomas from the Smithsonian Institution explored "the most interesting and extensive works to be found in the state of West Virginia," consisting of fifty mounds along the Kanawha River, surrounding the village of Spring Hill (Kanawha County).[9] The eleventh mound examined, measuring thirty-five by forty feet at its base and four feet tall, revealed a particular surprise.

In the center, three feet below the surface, was a vault eight feet long and three feet wide. In the bottom of this, among the decayed fragments of bark wrappings, lay a skeleton fully seven feet long, extended at full length on the back, head west. Lying in a circle immediately above the hips were fifty-two perforated shell disks about an inch in diameter and one-eighth of an inch thick. The bones of the left arm were lying

THE KANAWHA COUNTY MOUND THAT REVEALED A GIANT SKELETON IN 1884.

Credit: Author's collection

along the side of the body, but those of the right were stretched out horizontally at right angles to the body, the bones of the hand touching a small conical mass of earth, which proved to be a kind of vault similar to that in the Criel mound (No. 1) above described. This was formed of a mortar or cement, but the contents, which must have been animal or vegetable, were completely destroyed. It was yet unbroken and barely large enough to have covered a squatting skeleton.[10]

An even larger skeleton was found in Mound 21, labeled the Great Smith mound, at a depth of nineteen feet. Enclosed in the remains of a bark coffin, that skeleton measured seven feet, six inches tall and nineteen inches wide across the shoulders. Each bony wrist bore six heavy copper bracelets, and a copper gorget—protective collar—lay upon the chest. Three other skeletons were found within the mound, one "rather large," the rest of normal size.[11]

Mound 31 contained two normal-sized skeletons, plus two that were "very large," though Professor Thomas provided no measurements. The latter were buried "in a sitting position, facing each others, with their extended legs interlocking to the knees. Their hands, outstretched and slightly elevated, were placed in a sustaining position to a hemispherical, hollowed, coarse-grained sandstone, burned until red and brittle."[12]

Professor Thomas investigated other sites that year, as well. Five miles above the mouth of the Kanawha River, on a farm owned by Charles McCulloch, he discovered a mound that, despite long cultivation, still measured twenty feet high and 300 feet in circumference. A rock pile at its apex had already been "disturbed by parties who found a very large skeleton with some stone weapons."[13] Thomas offered no opinion on the giant skeletons. Their origin and reason for their burial with aborigines of normal size is unexplained today. ■

ANCIENT WALKERS?

IN 1896 THE *American Anthropologist* published a short item on the last page of its February issue, reading:

Fossil Footprint—It is reported that H. E. Huford, of Kemper Lane, Walnut Hills, Cincinnati, exhibited before a recent meeting of the Ohio State Academy of Science, a large stone taken from the hillsides four miles north of Parkersburg, on the West Virginia side of the Ohio river: about twenty years ago, in which there was the imprint of a perfect human foot, 14½ inches in length. The matter will be investigated by the Society.[14]

No follow-ups appeared, a regrettable lapse that has not prevented Internet bloggers from filling in the gaps. A mystical website, titled "Pure Insight," claims "one expert has calculated from the type of rock depicted, and its position on the river's edge, that the track must be at least 150 million years old, according to modern geologic dating."[15] Other sites echo that estimate of age, but none has so far managed to identify the "expert" or present any corroborating evidence.

Designation of a "giant" footprint is problematic. As a rule of thumb—or toe—the length of a person's foot is normally about fifteen percent of his or her height. Thus, all things being equal, a man with a 14½-inch foot should stand eight feet, eight inches tall. That said, Robert Wadlow's feet measured 18½ inches at maturity, while he was 8 feet, 11.1 inches tall, meaning that his foot's length equaled 19.2 percent of his height.

If the Parkersburg footprint existed—and others like it have been faked or misinterpreted, as at Paluxy, Texas[16]—we may assume that the person who made it qualified for "giant" status. As to the footprint's suggested extreme antiquity, the wait for proof continues. ∎

>> CENTRAL CITY & WHEELING

ON JUNE 23, 1908, readers of the *Washington Post* were treated to an article headlined "GIANT IN ANCIENT MOUND. Curious Relics of Prehistoric Times Is [*sic*] Found in the Tomb." The article read:

Huntington W. Va., June 22—The municipal authorities of Central City, four miles west of here, three weeks ago ordered the removal of a prehistoric mound from Thirteenth street. Today twelve feet above the base of the mound a gigantic human skeleton was discovered. It was almost seven feet in length and of massive proportions.

It was surrounded by a mass of rude trinkets. Eight huge copper bracelets were discovered. These, when burnished, proved to be of purest beaten copper and a perfect preservation. Rude stone vessels, hatchets, and arrow heads were found with the skeleton.

A curiously inscribed totem was found at the head of the skeleton. The Smithsonian Institution will be notified of the discovery.[17]
Again, no follow-up was published, but more giant remains surfaced five months later, this time at Wheeling. According to

The Afro-American, *dated December 5, 1908:*

*Prof. E. L. Lively and J. L. Williamson, of Friendly, has [**sic**] made an examination of the giant skeletons found by children playing near that town. The femur and vertebrae were found to be in a remarkable state of preservation and showed the person to be of enormous stature. The skeletons ranged in height from seven feet, six inches down to six feet, seven inches. The skulls found are of peculiar formation. The forehead is low and slopes back gradually, while the back part of the head is very prominent, much more so than the skulls of people living at the present day. The legs are exceedingly long and the bones unusually large. The finding of the skeletons has created a great deal of interest and the general impression is that the bones are the remains of the people who built the mounds, the largest in the county being located at Moundsville, Marshall County.[18]*

What became of those remarkable relics is anyone's guess. ∎

ALIVE & KICKING?

WEST VIRGINIA KEEPS no formal roster of its tallest residents, but one visitor described by UFO researcher Earl Wayne Menefee would shatter all world records if proved accurate. According to Menefee, the giant sighting occurred "back around the late 1940s or early 1950s," on Chatham Hill, east of Farmington in Marion County.

On the night in question, two unnamed women—deemed "credible witnesses" by Menefee—were chatting outside their homes, waiting for their husbands to return from a late shift at a coalmine, between 11:30 p.m. and midnight. Suddenly, they saw a bizarre male figure approaching, clad in a long, shiny, green robe, with a red cap perched atop its head. That head "was up under the old street light flange" according to Menefee, pegging the figure's height around twelve to fifteen feet. The terrified women fled to their respective homes and never saw the giant again.[19]

Menefee considered the sighting a UFO-related event but, while Chatham Hill has been the locus of multiple UFO sightings, neither witness to the strangely dressed giant's appearance described any aerial lights or other strange phenomena. The link remains speculative, and the sighting itself is uncorroborated, with one witness deceased by 1994.

Another unverified tale comes from Internet blogger E. T. Babinski, quoting former "young Earth" evangelist Kent Hovind. According to Babinski, Hovind told his followers, "Someone in the audience at one of my creation seminars came up to me and told how they or someone they knew was working in a mine in West Virginia or Kentucky, and they found a 'giant human skeleton' in the mine, but no one was interested enough to excavate the bones or investigate further, and the whole area was then covered beneath water because they built a dam in that region."[20]

Such vague tales were Hovind's stock in trade as an minister prior to his November 2006 conviction on federal tax evasion charges, resulting in a ten-year prison sentence.[21] The holder of a disputed Ph.D.—widely known as "Dr. Dino" for his claims that humans shared the Earth with dinosaurs 4,000 to 6,000 years ago—Hovind was criticized even by other "young Earth" creationist groups such as Kentucky's Answers in Genesis, who found his "Hovind Theory" of Noah's Ark dodging a giant ice meteor (-300° Fahrenheit) "fraudulent."[22] Hovind's Dinosaur Adventure Land theme park, opened in 2001, banked an estimated $1 million per year for Hovind prior to his arrest, most of which he tried to hide from tax collectors.[23]

Clearly, Hovind's word cannot be trusted. As for the other reports of giants found, then lost in West Virginia, conspiracy theories surround their disappearance, hypothesizing a long cover-up by the Smithsonian Institution in Washington. The museum's motive, presumably, is to avert potentially catastrophic disruption of established scientific theories or religious faith, with the inevitable impact on America's economy and government.[24]

Fact or paranoia? Lacking further evidence, the mystery, while titillating, shall remain unsolved. ∎

CHAPTER 8

BIGFOOT

When most people think of the cryptid called Bigfoot or Sasquatch, they picture a creature lumbering through woodlands of the Pacific Northwest. And, it's true, a huge number of sightings have emerged from that region over time: 937 from Oregon, Washington, and British Columbia, according to the Bigfoot Field Researchers Organization (BFRO), without adding reports from northern California.[1]

Most Americans, however, do not realize that every US state except Hawaii has its share of Bigfoot sightings on file, ranging from a low of five (Rhode Island) to triple digits in some surprising locations: 272 in Florida, 253 in Ohio, 247 in Illinois, 199 in Texas, 185 in Michigan, 116 in Georgia, 115 in Colorado, 113 in Missouri, 102 in Pennsylvania, 100 in New York.[2]

In short, it seems Bigfoot is everywhere.

As for West Virginia, there is no consensus among researchers. The BFRO lists ninety-two encounters from the Mountain State, while other websites, books, and articles cite lower numbers, but refer to cases missed by the BFRO. After reviewing all available sources, my tally includes 162 eyewitness sightings of Bigfoot-type creatures, twenty-nine discoveries of oversized, humanoid footprints, and 116 other incidents involving strange sounds or smells, objects thrown at humans, and other events theoretically linked to Bigfoot. ∎

**ANONYMOUS HOAXED PHOTO
OF A BIGFOOT ALLEGEDLY KILLED
SOMETIME IN 1894.**

>> EARLY ENCOUNTERS

MANY STATES HAVE aboriginal Bigfoot traditions dating from pre-Columbian times, or reports from pioneering settlers. West Virginia's first reports, by contrast, are relatively recent, dating from the early 1900s and only brought to light in May 2006. The events, all allegedly occurring in Pocahontas County, began with a sighting by multiple loggers at their forest camp, where they saw "a large light-gray-haired man like creature running along the tops of the log piles." Sometime later, "something" dragged a mule under a cattle gate, leaving it dead and mutilated. When the farmer found his mangled animal, he heard heavy breathing and footsteps in frozen snow that "sounded like a huge man." Finally, a hunter "saw something in a tree," waiting years past the event to describe it as "the devil."[3]

On September 6, 1925, the *Charleston Gazette* published the following short item from Buckhannon, seat of Upshur County.

The report last week that a wild ape was roaming the country near the Wesleyan camp proved to be an exciting subject for the footballers; but when a party was suggested to be formed including some of the squad, to capture the ape, Coach Russ put an end to the monkey business.[4]

And to reports of the elusive "ape" as well, apparently. No follow-ups were published.

Skip forward to the early 1930s, date unknown. A report from the International Bigfoot Society (IBS) website describes a clash between Bigfoot and a group of moonshiners on Little Hearts Creek, near Chapmanville (Logan County). The whiskey cookers fled their still, pursued by Bigfoot, but escaped when the creature became tangled up in an old barbed wire fence.[5]

Another decade passed before our next report, from the 1940s. Wayne County residents reported sightings of a "headless man," prompting a modern correspondent to surmise that they saw Bigfoot, known from descriptions as having a relatively small head and "no neck."[6] A stretch, perhaps, but no less likely than headless corpse roaming at large. ∎

>> THE 1950S

THE "HAPPY DAYS" ERA produced three reports. The first sighting, from Pocahontas County, occurred in spring or early summer of 1952, on US Route 219, two miles south of Buckeye. A driver passing through at 1:15 a.m. saw a hairy biped, roughly five feet, six inches tall, cross the highway in front of his car and duck into a roadside ravine.[7]

At 9:30 p.m. on December 15, 1959, a young Brooke County trapper checking his lines near State Route 2 met "a large hairy creature," perhaps six feet tall and "very large in stature," with yellow eyes and bared teeth. The youth fled in panic, leaping from a cliff into a snow bank. He returned the next morning and found tracks, "not very clear but they were large."[8]

Our last report from the Fifties is undated beyond reference to the decade, coming from the same Wayne County witness who reported the earlier sightings of "headless men." Call her "Witness X." In this case, one of her in-laws was hanging wash out to dry when she saw "a large, black and hair covered creature on two legs, move from the hillside and cross the road above their farmhouse," near East Lynn Lake.[9] ∎

▶ SWINGING SIXTIES

THIS DECADE'S ENCOUNTERS began with a summer sighting near Davis, in Tucker County. Several young men were camped out, one chopping firewood, when he found himself facing a "horrible monster." He said, "It had two huge eyes that shone like big balls of fire, and we had no light at all. It stood every bit of eight feet tall and had shaggy long hair all over its body. It just stood and stared at us. Its eyes were very far apart."[10]

Author Rick Berry reports the same or a similar creature prowling around Davis from 1960 to 1975, "frequently seen by campers, hikers and horseback riders," but regrettably, he offers no specifics.[11]

That same summer, around Parson (Tucker County), British authors Janet and Colin Bord report that "many" witnesses reported sightings of an eight-foot, hairy biped with eyes "like big balls of fire."[12] It is tempting to suggest that the Bords simply garbled the report from Davis—missing from their timeline of Bigfoot sightings—but Parson and Davis lie seventeen miles apart, and Rick Berry cites encounters from both areas.[13]

Nineteen-sixty ends with an October report from motorist W. C. "Doc" Priestly. While driving through the Monongahela National Forest, Priestly's car died suddenly, near Marlinton (Pocahontas County). "Then I saw it," Priestly told the *Charleston Daily Mail*. "To my left beside the road stood this monster with long hair pointing straight up toward the sky." Friends of Priestly, traveling ahead of him by bus, turned back on noticing that he was no longer behind them. As they reached him, Priestly said, "It seemed this monster was very much afraid of the bus and dropped his hair, and to my surprise, as soon as he did this, my car started to run again. The thing took off when the bus stopped."[14]

Priestly kept the story to himself and proceeded on his way, trailing the bus. Soon, his car began to fail again. "I could see the sparks flying out from under the hood as if it had a very bad short," he said. "And sure enough, there beside the road stood the monster again." Once more, the bus returned and Bigfoot fled, leaving the points of Priestly's engine "completely burned out."[15]

Such tales—sometimes including UFOs and psychic Sasquatches—infuriate some "flesh-and-blood" researchers who believe that Bigfoot is a giant ape or proto-human, nothing more. And yet, year after year, we hear more reports that seem to challenge mere zoology. Are witnesses to those events all liars, or insane?

You be the judge.

No creature was seen on Clutts Hill Road near Lesage (Cabell County), on November 15, 1960, but witness "Ron B." believes he heard one howling in the forest, while hunting with his grandfather and a friend. He described that howl as "the most bloodcurdling sound I have ever heard," rendered in his report to

MONONGAHELA NATIONAL FOREST HAS PRODUCED MULTIPLE BIGFOOT SIGHTINGS.

Credit: US National Park Service

the BFRO as "AHH-EEE-EEE-EEE," followed by "a deep-throated growl that lasted about five seconds."[16]

At 11 p.m. on December 30, 1960, bakery truck driver Charles Stover saw "a monster, standing erect, with hair all over its body" near Hickory Flats, between Braxton and Webster Counties. Other locals reported strange cries in the woods around the same time, blaming "the Braxton Beast."[17]

Our next report dates from June 1961 but was not reported until December 2012. Witness "S. P." was prowling the woods near Huntington with best friend Bill Roberts when they met "an animal neither of us recognized." First seen crouching, the black-haired biped rose to a "very tall" height, whereupon the boys noted it was "skinny in appearance with a tapered face."[18]

In November 1966, during the Mothman flap, Cecil Lucas saw three "bear-like creatures" sniffing around an oil pump on his Mason County property, near Point Pleasant. As he approached to investigate, they fled toward the Ohio River, running on their hind legs. Local sightings resumed in 1968, with hairy bipeds seen crossing highways, approaching cars parked on Lover's Lane, and lurking around the TNT Area.[19]

The decade closed with three more encounters from 1969. That summer, "Rod A." and his wife were staying overnight with cousin "Buck" at his home, thirty miles south of Chapmanville, when a shaggy beast reached through the bedroom window, trying to drag Rod's wife outside, finally relenting when they screamed and bent its arm.[20] In August, two sisters walking to a rural store in McDowell

County saw a "gangly" seven-foot biped with patchy hair on its back in Shop Hollow.[21] On November 24, father-son hunters saw Bigfoot near the Greenbrier River, outside Marlinton. According to the boy:

It was a very large animal about seven foot tall...There was very little hair on the face and I remember thinking he looked like the very kind and wise black gentleman that my father knew. It had brown hair with streaks of red, and a dark brown face with very dark eyes, but not "without Soul." Its hair, not fur, did not seem to be matted or nasty.[22]

Three final cases from the 1960s bear no specific dates. In Wayne County, two cousins saw "a very large hairy thing" rise from a river beside their canoe, prompting one frightened youth to break a paddle over its head. Later, one of the cousins says "a very large hairy thing with red eyes" pursued him on land, in the same vicinity.[23] Meanwhile, near Hurricane (Putnam County), an eight-year-old saw an apelike creature "up a tree eating acorns." Neighbors reported noises from the woods that "sounded like Arabs in prayer."[24] ■

THE 1970S

BIGFOOT SIGHTINGS ESCALATED in the "Feel Good Decade." In summer of 1971, a brother of busy Witness X saw "something very large, dark, and hairy" cross a Wayne County road with one astounding leap. Despite its speed, he noted the creature's "bloody red" eyes, branding it "a devil."[25]

Our next anonymous witness, a firefighter, met Bigfoot on Knipetown Road, seven miles north of Martinsburg (Berkeley County). He recalls the date—March 30—but could only place the incident within the "early 1970s." The creature was eight to nine feet tall, with a "very heavy build, long lanky arms, long dark red hair, [and a] very long stride," crossing the road in three steps.[26]

On May 1, 1974, a Harrison County teenager met Bigfoot while collecting nightcrawlers as fishing bait. Seen from sixty feet, the "enormous animal...built like a body builder" stood about nine feet tall and had long hair dangling from its forearms.[27] Dates are vague for a farmer's sighting from the fringe of Jackson County's Frozen Camp Wildlife Management Area. Sometime in 1974 or '75, while checking his livestock, the witness saw "a big monkey in a tree."[28]

We have more details for two sightings from July 1975. First, on July 14, a child playing in a Logan County creek near his home saw a creature six to seven feet tall, "covered in thick black fur and it stood upright, broad at the shoulders, [with] long arms."[29] In Raleigh County, date unknown, three youths met Bigfoot outside Beckley. They report being stalked by a "black shape" that rolled large boulders "the size of a washer or drier" downhill, onto their forest path.[30]

The mid-1970s produced another child's report from Cranesville (Preston County). While riding with an older brother and sister, the witness says something "tall and hairy but fast" pursued their pickup truck, "swooping" over the truck's bed before it retreated.[31]

In June 1976, brothers "Randy" and "Gary" went camping at Bluestone State Park (Summers County) to celebrate Gary's high

BLUESTONE STATE PARK.

Credit: US National Park Service

school graduation. They were troubled overnight by high-pitched vocalizations and sounds of breaking tree limbs. Next morning, exploring, they found an "unnatural" clearing in the forest, "made by pushing over and breaking off trees." Inside the clearing, "vegetation had been laid in a random fashion on the ground roughly six inches thick."[32] Breakage of trees and limbs is a common component of Bigfoot encounters.

One month later, a nine-year-old witness and his grandmother heard "this awful high pitched scream...like a woman being attacked or murdered" at their Preston County home, outside Manown. Aiming a flashlight beam toward the woods, they saw "two sets of huge red eyes" staring back.[33]

On August 17, 1976, teenagers Clifford Barnes and Ronald Stark were approaching a drive-in theater on Skin Creek Road, in Weston, when they saw a black simian figure crouched on the pavement. Seeing them, it rose to full height—about eight feet—and watched them for thirty seconds before ambling into the woods. The youths reported their sighting to the county sheriff.[34]

On November 23, 1978, a deer hunter saw Bigfoot near Hile Run Road, outside St. George (Tucker County). His description reads:

Appeared very tall. Arms extended below his knees. Long brown shaggy hair. Hair at his head appeared to be longer as if it came to his shoulders. Pug face from side

THE CLOSEST MOST AMERICANS WILL EVER COME TO BIGFOOT, A GARDEN STATUE SOLD BY DESIGN TOSCANO.

view. Long legs and long stride. Four to five feet stride (measured by my boot length).[35]

Later, speaking to a BFRO investigator, he added that the creature was six to seven feet tall, "lanky and thin," weighing 200 pounds or less.[36]

During the winter of 1978-79, a family living two miles west of Mannington (Marion County) reported serenades of "strange howls and screams" around their rural home on successive nights. One evening, an unseen prowler tore down the home's outdoor drainpipes, leaving large manlike footprints behind.[37]

Sometime in 1978 or '79, the same farmer who saw Bigfoot near the Frozen Camp Wildlife Management Area four years earlier logged a second sighting, one-quarter mile from the first encounter's location. This time, his son also saw the tall, dark brown biped that "was not a man or a bear."[38]

On August 10, 1979, twelve members of a Mercer County family saw Bigfoot peering through a window of their rural home, eight miles from Princeton. Four men grabbed shotguns and fired at the creature, said to have "small greenish yellow eyes," but it escaped.[39]

An e-mail correspondent from Wayne County, residing near Fort Gay, reports multiple incidents of "long, moanful, howling noises coming from the woods on the hill that faced our house." The first were heard in 1979, followed by repetitions every autumn through 1984.[40]

A final report, dated from June in the "late 1970s," involves two men gigging frogs on a farm near Milton. Splashing sounds drew their attention to a gray-haired "animal creature bending down at the creek, drinking water out of its hands." Startled by their flashlights, it rose and fled, "running on two legs like a man."[41] ■

>> THE 1980S

OUR FIRST REPORT for this decade dates from summer of 1980, reported by witness "Dwayne W." He saw no creature during his night-fishing trip with a friend, at Huntington's Spring Valley, but heard sounds "like people talking backwards," followed by "a hair-raising, blood-curdling SCREAM from just up the hill behind us." In passing, Dwayne recalls his family's encounter with a grunting "red-eyed monster" years earlier, but offers no further details.[42]

Screams also announced Bigfoot's presence in Logan County, on April 15, 1982, but a young witness saw the beast that time, from twenty-five feet. He says, "It was black, about eight feet tall, and walking on two legs. It ran

up into the mountainside and I never saw or heard it again." An aged neighbor recognized that description, relating it to a "dog man" he saw "years ago."[43]

In September 1982, five teenagers from Fort Gay were idling at an old cemetery on Hewlett Branch Road, when huffing, grunting sounds disturbed them. A seven-foot figure appeared, scaring them back to their car. Headlights revealed a brown-furred biped that "looked like a pro basketball player," shielding its eyes and swiftly retreating. Years later, one witness said the beast's vocalizations were "the same long, mournful sounds" recorded on the BFRO's website.[44]

A report vaguely dated from the "early

Eighties" describes a sighting from Pleasant Dale, in Hampshire County. Several boys were hunting small game at the old town dump, when one saw Bigfoot through his rifle's scope and urged the others to leave. He refused to hunt around the dump thereafter, but only explained his reason two decades later.[45]

In June 1983, a group of college students hiking through Pipestem Resort State Park, on the border of Mercer and Summers Counties, heard "a loud, bone-chilling scream just above us, slightly behind us, no more than forty to fifty feet away." They fled the scene, one later writing, "The scream is hard to describe because I can't compare it to anything. It was incredibly loud and menacing. It wasn't 'pure'—it had texture."[46]

In August 1983, a third report emerged from Frozen Camp Wildlife Management Area. A college student camping out was wakened by "an animal call I had never heard before. I can only describe the sound by saying it was big and had the lung capacity of a lion or an elephant. It literally shook the forest and my chest." Frightened, he fled the area in darkness, with only his dog, a knife, and a flashlight, leaving behind his tent and other gear.[47]

A similar event occurred in Webster County, on the night of July 12, 1985. Two friends camped at Glade Run Pond, in the Monongahela National Forest, heard loud "wooooooooop-woop-woop-woop" sounds repeated several times. Next morning, they found their can of lighter fluid neatly covered with a pyramid of rocks, near their tent. Later that day, an unseen watcher stole a string of fish they caught for dinner.[48]

Our next report also comes from the Monongahela National Forest, near Canaan Valley. Three campers saw two hairy bipeds

PIPESTEM RESORT STATE PARK.

prowling the woods around 11:30 p.m. on July 4, 1987, one of the creatures walking with a limp. Reporting to the BFRO, one witness wrote, "The thing that overwhelmed me was when I shined the flashlight in its face, the eyes were yellow, the exact same color as a deer's eyes at night. That told me that this thing was nocturnal."[49] (In fact, deer roam and feed at all hours of the day and night. Yellow eyeshine, seen in birds, cats, and dogs, does not dictate a nocturnal lifestyle.)

A second sighting on July 4, 1987, was reported from Wyoming County, near Hanover. Twenty relatives celebrated with fireworks that night, and they were roasting hotdogs when an eight-foot-tall biped crashed the party, "grunting with a low growl." Several witnesses noted a smell "like urine and a nasty baby diaper," before two men approached the creature with a pistol. It hurled a stick at them, then "screamed like a woman and ran into the woods" with bullets flying around it. "The scream," one witness wrote, "seemed to be as loud as a train horn."[50]

Nicholas County also produced a sighting in July, date unknown. Witness "D. A." and two friends were swimming at Krofford Hole on the Gauley River, when their noise attracted "a large two-legged animal, dark brown in color." It stood watching them, silently, for about two minutes, then retreated into the forest. D. A. measured nearby trees, estimating the creature's height at seven feet.[51]

Two more sightings from 1987 come to us undated. A resident of Basin (Wyoming County) saw a large "shadow" in the woods, mistaking it for his hunting companion until he recognized an arm with long dangling hair.[52] In Lincoln County, two hikers found "what appeared to be a bedding area" made from limbs as thick as a man's arm, snapped from trees six to eight feet off the ground. Questioning locals, they found several who had seen a hairy "goat boy" in the area.[53]

In 2006, a hunter from Monongalia County

MONONGAHELA NATIONAL
FOREST, SCENE OF MULTIPLE
BIGFOOT SIGHTINGS.

Credit: US National Park Service

MONSTERS

informed the BFRO of several presumed Bigfoot encounters, both personal and claimed by others. His first experience occurred on May 10, 1988, when a large unseen stalker trailed him along a railroad grade, complete with sounds of "loud heavy branches breaking and heavy footfalls that I know could not have been a deer or bear." A year later, that incident was repeated in the same vicinity. The witness also said his mobile home "has been slapped on several occasions with great force," waking him from sleep. Once, he saw three bipedal silhouettes pass his bedroom window, ranging in height from eight feet to six feet, six inches. Finally, he recalled a friend from Buckhannon who found a pile of dead deer, neatly stacked, all gutted, with their necks and legs broken.[54]

On November 23, 1989, two deer hunters saw a pair of shaggy bipeds from their separate tree stands, near Elkwater (Randolph County). One creature was five feet tall, foul smelling, covered with matted reddish-brown hair, possessing visible humanoid finger- and toenails. Its companion was black, eight to nine feet tall, with "very human-like features but a different nose." The creatures chattered back and forth, making gestures that were "extremely human-like," then retreated through the forest, howling loudly.[55]

Witness X from Wayne County caps the decade with four reports dating "some twenty years" prior to 2009. One incident involved an unseen prowler in the woods, whistling and shrieking "like a woman screaming." Around the same time, Witness X and two of her brothers lost watchdogs, each found strangled or with broken necks, spines and legs snapped in two cases, otherwise unmarked.[56] ■

>> THE 1990S

AS WITNESS X CLOSED the previous decade, so she opened the Nineties with a report from two of her brothers. The men were riding ATVs in Wayne County when "something just seemed to 'float' up from some tall weeds near them, and the thing that really scared them was the height and the eyes. It was very, very tall and the eyes were green, about the size of golf balls, and spaced some four to six inches apart. They said they seemed to glow!"[57]

One summer night in 1990, a witness walking home at 8:30 p.m. saw a large bipedal creature moving among tombstones at Marmet Memorial Gardens Cemetery (Kanawha County). He told the BFRO, "It would stop sometimes as if to dig at a grave. It was very large, dark hairy appearance, ape like movements, shrugging of the shoulders and sometimes a hop to its step."[58]

On August 10, 1990, Bigfoot revealed itself to a night-shift security guard at a strip mine on 22 Mine Road, six miles southwest of Logan (Logan County). The witness first mistook it for a black bear, then recognized "a large bipedal animal" that shielded its face from his flashlight beam "with huge hands" before running away on two legs.[59]

In early October 1989, two hunters stalking deer near Wildell (Pocahontas County) "freaked out" after finding three humanoid footprints, each five inches longer than a man's size 10½ boot—i.e., approximately fifteen inches long. They also crossed paths with another hunter who had seen two huge "upright figures" moving through the woods.[60]

In June 1991, an anonymous married couple purchased a long-abandoned farm near Milton. Soon, wild, outlandish howling from the

SENECA CREEK BACKCOUNTRY.

woods disturbed their nights, convincing the tenants that "something was out there."[61]

Wayne County's Witness X supplies another tale, this one from 1994. Her son enjoyed off-road motorcycling, but once complained that "something that sounded very large growled at him," audible over the sound of his bike's engine. On another jaunt, he found something like a children's fort made of logs, at a remote location with no families nearby. Witness X attributes both incidents to Bigfoot.[62]

On June 15, 1994, a nine-year-old resident of Quiet Dell (Harrison County) reported "very high-pitched screams, like a woman being injured," accompanied by thrashing in the nearby underbrush. The GCBRO includes this case in its database, while admitting that other wildlife could have caused the sounds.[63]

At 2:30 a.m. on August 15, 1994, two fourteen-year-old boys set out to meet their girlfriends in the wilds of Raleigh County. They had trudged for several miles before a hairy biped blocked their path. A decade later, one witness wrote, "The thing that stuck in my mind all these years was its fingers. They were human like but much longer. They were at least three times as long. This creature was at least seven feet tall while it was hunched over."[64]

On October 15, 1994, a father and son hiking through the Sherwood Lake Recreation Area (Greenbrier County) saw "two very large black upright creatures ripping branches and bark from the trees. It appeared that they were eating the bark." On another occasion, while free-diving at Sherwood Lake, the adult witness found "numerous large tracks crossing shallow areas of the lake in water up to eight feet deep."[65]

Four Pocahontas County hunters also had a series of encounters and near misses in October 1994. On the first day of their trip, one saw two hairy bipeds, six to seven feet tall, walk past his tree stand. On day three,

THE DOLLY SODS REGION OF
MONONGAHELA NATIONAL FOREST.

MONSTERS

witness "Scott" found four humanoid footprints on a dirt logging road; they measured twenty-two inches long and eight inches wide, separated by a six-foot stride. On day four, Scott killed and dressed a buck, then left to fetch reinforcements for retrieving it. When the hunters returned, both the deer and its "gut pile" were missing, the carcass apparently "carried and NOT dragged" up a steep hillside.[66]

On November 5, 1994, seven spelunkers camped in Pendleton County's Seneca Creek Backcountry were disturbed by a single piercing cry "like a mammal, reminiscent of a woman's scream, but nothing like a cat's scream." Later, six miles from the campsite, two members of the party found a cave partially sealed off by boulders, but still accessible. Inside lay a doe's carcass, gnawed to the bone on its rear legs, its entrails and much of the soft tissue missing. Deer hair was also strewn around the floor and walls.[67]

Sometime in autumn 1994, several children were camped behind one boy's home in Nicholas County. Around 11:30 p.m., one boy's dog began growling inexplicably. Seconds later, a large hand pressed against their tent from outside. Years afterward, one witness wrote, "I could definitely see four fingers and an opposable thumb, and we all thought it was an adult man. We screamed and the hand pulled back." In fact, the only adult present that night was one boy's mother, and the nearest neighbor lived at least a mile away. Still, the boys convinced themselves that they were victims of a human prank, only reporting it as a possible Bigfoot encounter in 2008.[68]

On September 1, 1995, a married couple hiking through Pocahontas County heard whistling and caught a "wet hair smell," then briefly glimpsed a dark brown biped nine to ten feet tall before it turned and fled into the woods.[69]

In August 2012, the West Virginia Bigfoot Research Association's website announced a late-breaking report from 1995, of events occurring somewhere in "the northern part of the state." Webmaster "Rick" asked readers to "stay tuned" for further information, but none has been posted so far.[70]

On October 11, 1996, two workmen were clearing brush at a camp near Spruce Knob—West Virginia's tallest peak, at 4,863 feet—when they heard "these amazing noises, yelling, screaming, loud squealing," followed by sounds "like a large person tearing through the woods." They saw no creatures, but agreed the sounds were unlike any either man had previously heard.[71]

Around midnight on November 15, 1996, three teenagers were driving aimlessly along the border between Lewis and Harrison Counties. They stopped to relieve themselves, and were thus engaged "when out of nowhere something jumped off of the bank and landed in the road about twenty to twenty-five feet behind us." The creature "screamed like a crazy woman," but was still too far away for them to see it as they fled.[72]

That same month, a Cabell County hunter was stalking deer at 5:30 a.m. when a roaring animal hurled a tree branch at him, striking him in the back and knocking him down. Again, the creature passed unseen, but its victim "firmly believe[d] that the animal walked away on two legs and from the force of the steps was heavy in weight."[73]

On September 23, 1997, Scott Sharp found humanoid tracks "too large to be human" near Forest Road 75, in the Dolly Sods section of Monongahela National Forest. The footprints measured twenty inches long. That night, while camped, he heard "loud, piercing screams" and smelled "a strange odor, like a cross between a skunk and sweat." Sharp found more tracks around his camp the next morning, with freshly broken tree branches.[74]

David Johannson heard what he thought was Bigfoot on December 1, 1997, while hunting with his son in the Cranberry Wilderness near Richwood (Nicholas County).

The creature cried like "a woman screaming, followed by a strange sort of chatter, as if someone were playing a recording of a human-like conversation backwards."[75]

In late January of 1998, motorist Scott Fadely saw Bigfoot standing beside Route 55 in Pendleton County, near the Smoke Hole Resort at Seneca Rocks. The creature was "very tall, fuzzy looking, with primate features, similar to an ape." It stepped onto the highway, making Fadely swerve to avoid a collision.[76]

August 1998 brought multiple Bigfoot reports from Capels, in McDowell County. Two hunters saw an eight-foot-tall biped covered with long black hair, in separate incidents, and the BFRO's website refers to "many tracks found and terrible screams heard." A hearsay report also mentions a hunter found dead in the area. Police "allegedly ruled his death a homicide but said they have not been able to identify what killed him due to the markings and wounds on the body."[77]

Sometime in autumn 1998, a motorist reportedly saw Bigfoot cross the Kingwood Pike in Monongalia County, around 3 a.m., but further details are lacking.[78] In October of that year, e-mail correspondent "Rodney B." reported hearing "very unusual howls" on several occasions at Rocklick (Fayette County). A friend of Rodney's added his sighting of an eight-foot-tall biped seen crossing a nearby road.[79]

Members of an unidentified Marion County family claimed several Bigfoot encounters near Rivesville in April 1998. On April 21, two witnesses riding ATVs smelled a "horrible stench" and saw a hairy creature crouching beside a tree. That evening, three more family members met Bigfoot near the same location, this time walking upright, standing eight to nine feet tall. On April 23, two more relatives heard wood-knocking and "a high pitch hunting dog scream" while mushroom hunting in the same vicinity.[80]

In July 1999, two campers heard "howl-like sounds" in the Dolly Sods Wilderness, north of Seneca Rocks. Later that night, something prowled around their camp, leaving a humanoid footprint sixteen inches long and six inches wide.[81]

Two final sightings from the Nineties date vaguely from 1999. Two brothers hiking near Griffithsville (Lincoln County) found a "large" bare footprint in the woods, but took no measurements.[82] A more dramatic story comes from Bughurry Hollow (McDowell County), posted online by GCBRO member Rick Vereen. It read:

> I returned around 7 p.m. from church. I heard the dogs out back, raising Cain as if they were into a major fight, so I went to check on them. As I rounded the house a large creature grabbed me and threw me down like a limp rag. It was very strong. By the time I recovered, it was gone. Four of my dogs were killed, and the other was injured.[83] ∎

THE TWENTY-FIRST CENTURY

THE FIRST ALLEGED BIGFOOT REPORT OF 2000 came from Mount Porte Crayon, in the Roaring Plains Wilderness of the Monongahela National Forest (Randolph County), on July 15. Returning home from work that night, the witness was shocked by "the loudest, most intense scream I have ever heard in my life." He searched in vain, but

NEW RIVER GORGE.

later heard the screams on two more nights, while relatives sharing his home reported six similar incidents.[84]

Eight days later, a camper in the Dolly Sods Wilderness, north of the Red Creek Campground, saw a "person" walking through the woods nearby. The figure "was from head to toe in a seamless dark color, lighter than black and darker than brown. There was no gap of skin and it appeared the hands, neck and head were the exact same color as the body." Noticing the witness, he (or it) "tore off into the brush very quickly and where there is no trail."[85]

Rounding off July 2000 is a predawn incident from New River Gorge (Fayette County), where someone or something hurled a large stone onto the tin roof of an open platform at a campground. One of the campers on site, GCBRO member Rick Vereen, concluded

that the stone "either fell from the sky or was tossed from the mountainside behind us...as if whoever or whatever threw the rock was telling us to shut up and go to sleep." Surveying the nearby forest, Vereen photographed unusual tree markings, including "one that looks like a giant nest in the top of a big white pine." On two more weekend visits to the campsite, in September and October, Vereen heard wood-knocking sounds and discovered large, unidentifiable footprints.[86]

In August 2000, Bigfoot surprised three woodland hikers in Monongalia County, leaping from cover to land within arm's reach of them. The hikers fled, one retaining a mental image of the thing as being "nearly six feet tall, appeared albino, covered with short hair, and having a distinct man shape form. It didn't chase us or anything; I think it just wanted to give us a scare." He added two more sightings, of a dark-haired biped, reported by three other witnesses.[87]

On January 20, 2001, a group of fifteen persons riding ATVs near Point Pleasant found four large humanoid footprints, each sixteen to eighteen inches long and six to eight inches wide. One member of the group called DNR agents. A witness told the BFRO:

They sent one truck down to look at the print. This truck left and came back with about five more trucks...After they were done one of them stopped and told Jack that it was only a black bear print. I am no zoologist but I have seen black bear prints, and this was not one. There were no claw marks, but there were toes.[88]

Six days later, a quarter mile southwest of Cairo (Ritchie County), four visitors to an old, abandoned church found fifty sixteen-inch tracks in soft soil.[89]

In June 2001, a family living near Milton reported three disturbing incidents. First, the children found and photographed large manlike footprints near their home, described by their father as "nothing like I've seen before." A week later, their dog chased an unseen prowler and returned "covered in some kind of slimy stuff like slobber." Two days after that, "a very loud, long growl" outside the house sent their dog in pursuit once more, without success.[90]

On September 5, 2001, a father and son delivering newspapers along Route 3 in Talcott (Summers County) saw a hairy seven-foot biped with "long arms like a gorilla" plodding across one home's lawn.[91] Two weeks later, on September 19, several ATV riders stopping to relieve themselves heard some large creature moving through the underbrush. One later wrote, "Whatever it was, it was walking down the hill on two feet but it was no bear. We couldn't see anything but we could hear something breathing, so we just quietly backed

up and got on the four-wheelers and got the hell out of there."[92]

On October 15, 2001, an early morning birdwatcher from Elkins heard sounds "like a bear scratching against a tree only louder," then saw a hairy seven-foot biped with "the basic look of a man," shoulders slumped, and arms "almost reaching to the ground. It walked very slowly and many times stopped to straightened up and look around as if searching for something."[93]

One day later, in the Monongahela National Forest near Onego (Pendleton County), a nocturnal hunter heard rustling sounds and saw four pairs of yellow eyes reflecting his flashlight beam. A "skunky" odor filled the air, and some heavy object fell nearby, as if thrown at him, before the watchers melted into darkness.[94]

Another report emerged from Cairo on November 12, 2001. Four teenagers left choir practice at a rural church on Route 31 around 8:45 p.m., in time to see "a very tall and muscular looking figure" cross the road. It was "slightly hunched over, swinging its arms well below its thigh area, almost to the knees." Comparing it to nearby pine trees, the witnesses pegged its height between seven and eight feet.[95]

Strange sounds mark the new year's first alleged Bigfoot encounter, on March 23, 2002. While hunting fossils in Pocahontas County's portion of the Monongahela National Forest, the witness heard wood-knocking, a "very deep cough like noise," and "a higher pitch noise...kind of like squealing gibberish" that persuaded him to leave the area.[96]

Four months later, around 5:15 a.m. on July 22, a trucker met Bigfoot while driving on Route 10, along the Mingo-Logan County line. He told his brother of the sighting with some trepidation, whereupon the brother admitted seeing hairy bipeds "a few times" around nearby Ragland. After one such sighting, police allegedly found a mutilated cow in the pasture where Bigfoot was seen.[97]

While hiking on a neighbor's property near Pennsboro (Ritchie County), our next witness glimpsed Bigfoot jogging through the woods on August 13, 2002. At first, he thought the creature was a man dressed in brown coveralls, then realized the runner was seven to eight feet tall.[98]

The first encounter of 2003 occurred in Mason County on a February night. Dogs barking at the home of an off-duty policeman alerted him to "something" on his property, its movements marked by grunting sounds and bipedal footsteps crunching on snow, while trees toppled in its wake. Shortly before that incident, the officer and his wife had seen yellow eyeshine five feet above ground, while driving on a nearby country road.[99]

In spring of 2003, students on a class field trip northeast of Morgantown heard "a huge commotion" in the woods, "like a couple of huge guys romping around and making the Bard Owl [sic] call."[100] On July 12, a wildlife biologist heard "a very alarming call," consisting of multiple "whoops," on a logging lease owned by MeadWestvaco Corporation near Mabie (Randolph County).[101]

On November 27, 2003, a motorist nearly struck a large creature on US Route 50, near Burlington. She wrote:

I barely missed hitting it and as soon as I stopped I realized that this was definitely not a dog. It was too big. It was on the right side of the road, crossing to the left. It was black and walking on all fours, its front legs were longer than the back legs. I was petrified. I had no idea what it was. When it got to the left side of the road it turned and looked at me. Its eyes were glowing orange in my headlight.[102]

Interviewed by BFRO member Stephen Willis, the driver clarified her description,

JUDY GAP WHERE LARGE FOOTPRINTS APPEARED IN 2004.

saying that the beast resembled "an ape with human facial features." It never stood erect, but measured five to six feet tall on all fours. She said, "It was an animal, but it looked like it had intelligence behind its eyes."[103]

Another sighting on US Route 50 occurred on December 29, 2003, this one near Parkersburg (Wood County). The driver and one of his four passengers described the bipedal creature as eight feet tall, "brownish black, with long flowing hair." Reporting the incident online, the driver added an incident from 2001, when he found large tracks near his Ritchie County home. The footprints measured sixteen inches long, separated by a fifty-four-inch stride.[104]

Two more reports from 2003 bear no specific dates. In the first, two couples camped near Mossy glimpsed "somebody" standing near their tents, but the figure eluded their search.[105] In the other, from Raleigh County, a child told her parents she had been chased by "a bear" near their campsite. Around the same time, the parents noted "a horrible smell, sort of like wet fur, sweet fermented flowers with garbage mixed."[106] Such odors often accompany Bigfoot sightings.

On January 1, 2004, a family driving from Green Bank to Spruce Knob stopped beside a creek near Judy Gap (Pendleton County) and found bare footprints larger than a size 12 shoe (11¼ inches) in snow. On both feet, the second toe was longer than the others.[107]

On May 4, 2004, an Ohio County resident e-mailed the GCBRO, complaining that "for the past two weeks I have heard a strange moaning howl every night," accompanied by "a nasty wet dog, dead animal smell" and splashing from a nearby creek.[108]

On another May morning, before dawn, a driver saw Bigfoot standing between two houses on Mount Carmel Ridge, east of St. Marys (Pleasants County). "It was seven to eight feet tall," he wrote, "large, very hairy and dark in color standing on its back feet looking like a human figure, but very larger. It took off after about a minute and ran like lighting faster than any thing I have seen staying upright on its legs."[109]

One day in June 2004, a woman walking her dog on County Road 22 north of Middlebourne (Tyler County) heard wood-knocking, then dodged two stones hurled at her from the forest, followed by "the awfulest low growl then scream I have ever heard." Returning with her husband, she found a footprint that was "fairly large but shaped different."[110]

On October 5, near Bruceton Mills (Preston County), a couple saw a bear-sized creature standing on all fours, in their farmyard. Upon noticing them, it stood erect—about seven feet tall—and "walked mostly upright on two legs, swinging its arms and still looking at us until it turned its head to the hay field and walked away."[111]

On October 30, two Pocahontas County residents heard high-pitched hooting calls at Spruce Flats, three miles northwest of Marlinton. Nearby, they found a barbed wire fence knocked down. The father of one witness, on hearing the story, described his own encounter in the same vicinity, with an unseen thing that "smelled like a dirty, sweaty man who hadn't taken a bath in a few years."[112]

November 2004 brought a motorist's nocturnal sighting near Keyser (Mineral County), on Green Mountain Road. The creature was "at least 400 pounds and every bit of seven feet tall," covered in long brown hair that seemed "matted or dreadlocked." Before fleeing at the car's approach, it appeared to be watching a group of people gathered around a nearby bonfire.[113]

On December 12, 2004, Bigfoot visited Warwood, north of Wheeling (Ohio County), setting off a resident's motion-activated security lights at 1 a.m. The witness pegged its height

Credit: US National Park Service

THE GREENBRIER RIVER, SCENE OF A 1995 BFRO EXPEDITION.

at eight feet, "towering" over her bedroom window. She noted its muscular buttocks and "ratty coal black fur."[114]

Three months passed without another sighting. At 3:30 a.m. on March 13, 2005, the passenger in a car northbound on Interstate 77, nearing the Ohio border in Jackson County, briefly glimpsed a "very tall 'image' walking from right to left across this mountainside," apparently "covered somewhat with snow." His wife, at the wheel, saw nothing.[115]

In April 2005 the BFRO mounted an expedition along the Greenbrier River in Pocahontas County. On April 7th, team members heard howling familiar from tapes of other alleged Bigfoot calls. April 8th produced loud splashing from the river, as of heavy objects thrown into the water, but watchers saw nothing. On April 9th, something hurled a stick the size of a baseball bat at one of the searchers, followed by sounds of "something big climbing away." On April 13th, a searcher sighted two "tree-trunk dark" figures plodding through woods near the river.[116]

Beginning on May 30, 2005, a carpenter camped near his Barbour County worksite, between Belington and Philippi on Route 250, was awakened repeatedly by loud moaning sounds from the forest, sometimes accompanied by heavy "walking sounds." Searches by flashlight revealed nothing, and he never bothered looking for tracks.[117]

Around 10 p.m. on June 19, 2005, campers at the Wapacoma Campground, near Romney, woke to a series of loud "scream/wail/howl" sounds, gradually retreating while they heard "cows going nuts down that way on our side of the river."[118]

A month later, on July 22nd, a couple residing near Martinsburg (Berkeley County) saw two creatures in their backyard at 2 a.m. One stood upright, around seven feet tall; the other was first seen "on its hands and knees," perhaps sixteen inches high. The smaller

LAKE SHERWOOD.

Credit: US National Park Service

thing's fur "was not shaggy and appeared well groomed. It had blond hair on its belly and the rest was a darker red/brownish color. It crawled away at a startling speed in an army-like crawl," then rose and ran on two legs, its flight accompanied by "screams that sounded like a chimp."[119]

On October 10, 2005, four hunters camped near Hundred (Wetzel County) heard "possible" vocalizations and rock-clacking sounds. One witness wrote, "The screams sounded like a woman was being attacked. They sounded LOUD. The lungs that belted these screams out had to be huge."[120]

On November 23, 2005, an unnamed witness saw two "wild apes like Bigfoot" beside the Meadow River, near Route 60 (Greenbrier County). Three more showed up the following day, then left the area for parts unknown.[121]

On December 5th, a motorist saw two hairy bipeds six to seven feet tall, near Amigo (Wyoming County). As he described the event online:

It definitely wasn't a man or bear. All I know is it was walking upright. It did something that looked like it clapped its hands. Then I watched it kneel down and crawl into an airshaft for an abandoned mine. To my surprise, another one appeared out of nowhere and ran past it...The second one kneeled down and crawled into the same airshaft.[122]

On December 7th, a trail camera in Braxton County allegedly caught an unknown biped on film. The single photo, e-mailed to Loren Coleman by Frederick Gerwig, depicts a reddish-colored humanoid figure walking past trees, perhaps caught on infrared film.

Gerwig failed to explain the photo's color or poor quality beyond saying that the camera was "somewhat low tech to prevent theft."[123]

Five days later, a bicyclist stopping to relieve himself along State Route 18 near Sisterville (Tyler County) saw a large rock soar past him, hurled by an unseen assailant in the woods. He e-mailed a report to the BFRO on December 19.[124]

Our last report from 2005, undated, involves a Wayne County farmer shooting deer illegally to keep them from his garden. Once, while disposing of remains, he saw a "very large, what he thought was a wolf, watching him, hiding from the weeds," then revised his estimate upon hearing the beast utter a loud "scream/roar."[125]

The next report on file dates from February 2006. While hiking in Fayette County, the witness found "a bedding area. At first I thought it might have been made by deer or possibly other game, but there was a very foul stench associated with this area. I investigated a little further and found what I believe to be a large set of tracks leading to and away from this site." Returning to the spot a month later, he recorded high-pitched vocalizations and dodged a baseball-sized rock thrown from hiding.[126]

Two hunters heard "high-pitched whooping" in Nicholas County, on March 5, 2006, and replied with whoops of their own, producing calls that moved closer with "a different pattern to it." They left the area before the unseen yodeler arrived.[127]

Thirteen days later, a lone motorist met a strange creature while driving on Route 92 near Belington (Barbour County). He later wrote:

At first I thought it was a very tall, lanky human, at least six foot four, with long reddish hair and a long beard, but as I got closer, I realized there were no clothes, just reddish brown hair over its entire body.

The hair length and texture reminded me of a horse's groomed mane. The hair was smoothed and not matted, and my impression was that it was a very tall monkey type animal.[128]

On April 12, a Wyoming County turkey hunter encountered "something tall, black, hairy, and standing on two legs." At his approach, it fled into the woods.[129] May 11 brought a Preston County resident's report of four "quick, short, LOUD vocalizations" similar to purported Bigfoot calls recorded online. A neighbor heard "similar sounds, but more guttural" on May 25th.[130]

During that May's turkey season, two hunters saw Bigfoot near Clendenin, and one was about to shoot it when his partner stopped him. "Now I'm glad I didn't," the witness wrote. "Bigfoot is part of my Native American folklore."[131]

On July 16, 2006, a Calhoun County family went to feed one of their vacationing relative's dogs near Arnoldsburg. While there, their daughter began screaming, saying that a "little monkey" had growled at her, then ducked into the forest with its "mom." Later that night, she watched her father open the BFRO's website, displaying a picture of Bigfoot, and said, "That's the monkey I saw!"[132]

Less than two weeks later, on July 29th, three biologists surveying Boone County's bat population heard whooping cries at 2:30 a.m. and saw a large bipedal creature, some seven feet tall, cross a road near their camp. It was "completely covered in short, coarse-looking black hair except for its face, which was brown." After it fled, the men found "two distinct footprints, each much larger than any of our shoes."[133]

Late July also brought reports of repeated noisy visitations to a Mercer County farm, near Princeton. First, trees were found stripped of bark, exposing fresh-shredded wood underneath. Then came rock-clacking by night, and finally a "howling or moaning [that] first sounded like that of another type of animal in pain (more like a large pig or cow at first) but changed to sound like something 'very large' in size and getting very upset (VERY deep, angry tone growls)."[134]

On August 4th, the Preston County witness who heard strange sounds on May 11th reported another nocturnal serenade, presumably by Bigfoot.[135] Six days later, near Kenova (Wayne County), a mother and son traveling on Route 52 saw "a man" crossing the pavement, then realized the biped was not human.[136] On August 13th, campers at Audra State Park (Barbour County) noticed a foul smell, followed by wood-knocking and "a loud crashing noise, like a falling tree" in the forest.[137]

In early September 2006, witness "Helen" heard "a yelling noise and footsteps" near her Hampshire County home at 5 a.m. and looked outside, spotting two hairy bipeds standing side by side, one larger than the other. Her husband fired a gunshot, whereupon they fled.[138]

In the fourth week of September, a couple camped at Lake Sherwood in the Monongahela National Forest, reported an encounter with a "hoo hoo monster," so called for its loud hooting cries after nightfall.[139]

On October 8th, the same Hampshire County witness who reported seeing two creatures in early September claimed another sighting. This time, she said the beast was seven feet two inches tall, with "big yellow eyes." An added twist was her claim that "the family has seen a family of Sasquatches since first moving to the present home in the mid 1990s. She has seen them around the property over the years since she was six years old."

Credit: US National Park Service

RANDOLPH COUNTY'S OTTER CREEK WILDERNESS.

On October 23rd, the woman says a friend met an even larger biped, reportedly eight feet tall.[140]

The year closed with two reports from Pocahontas County. On October 30th, hikers reported a "possible vocalization and stalking" near Spruce Flats. That experience did not dissuade them from returning later in the year, date unknown, when they saw a hairy creature squatting in the woods. Its hair was "gray colored, almost white," and its eyes "reflected orange." Rising, it appeared to be eight feet tall, with "arms hanging below its knees."[141]

The year 2009 begins with a report from Randolph County's Otter Creek Wilderness, another portion of the Monongahela National Forest. Around 4:30 p.m. on January 9 or 10, while cutting firewood, two campers heard a loud warbling cry from the forest. "It wasn't a coyote," one wrote. "If it had been a coyote, it would have had to been at least 300 or 400 pounds to produce that kind of volume."[142]

Later the same week, at 11:30 p.m. on January 13th, Bigfoot revealed itself to a motorist driving on Route 55 near Seneca Rocks. The driver wrote:

It had long hair, what at first looked liked shredded material with clumps in it, hanging all off of its body...It seemed to have no neck, just a large head. I also realized it was very tall, and had very wide shoulders and its arms hung very low almost to its knees, if not below. It was walking or sort of trotting on hind legs like a man, but with a movement like an ape.[143]

Returning in daylight, the witness photographed several apparent footprints, but the photos remain unpublished.

On March 27th, a Marshall County farmer repairing his fence heard "sharp knocks replying" to his hammer blows from the nearby forest. Soon, the wood-knocking gave

way to "a chatter that sounded like native Indian language," frightening the farmer's dog.[144]

June 18, 2007, brought another nocturnal sighting from Route 55 near Seneca Rocks. This time, the driver and his daughter saw "two furry looking beings that appeared ape like but the fur was short." On seeing headlights, both creatures "took a big head first dive into those bushes" at roadside.[145]

Twelve days later, Bigfoot returned to the Monongahela National Forest, showing itself to a driver passing along the Cranberry River in Nicholas County. The witness recalls:

I saw what I thought at first was some idiot in a monkey suit in the middle of the road in front of me. I beeped my horn at it. He started to run very fast, in long strides and then I realized it wasn't a man. He wasn't wearing shoes. His feet looked hairy. He was covered in reddish brown hair and about six feet tall. The hair was all even in length. He ran about quarter of a mile up the hill in front of me then tore through some elderberry bushes and disappeared down the mountain.[146]

A hiker met Bigfoot at Seneca Rocks on July 6, 2007. It stood between six feet, six inches and seven feet tall, with visible "thick black hands and feet."[147] Two days later, on US Route 33 between Harmon and Seneca Rocks, a driver glimpsed "the hairiest thing I've ever seen" moving with "an ape-like walk, definitely not human." Its hair was "mossy grayish green color," and it "had no distinguishable facial features, because it was so hairy."[148]

A week passed before Bigfoot's next appearance, on July 15th, in Berkeley County. Two hikers described the beast as eight feet tall, black-haired, "stalking" them at an estimated running speed of thirty miles per hour. Even allowing for exaggeration, it was "way too fast to be a bear on two legs."[149]

On August 12th, a resident of Lindside (Monroe County) went to fetch the morning paper from her driveway and was shocked to meet a "big, tannish brown creature that had a sort of hump in its back. Its fur was short and clumped together." Fleeing to the house, she heard it banging on trees in the yard and wrote, "These bangings have been occurring quite frequently now."[150]

Around 6:15 p.m. on September 28th, two friends driving toward a farm outside Shady Springs (Raleigh County) saw "a HUGE 'something' standing above a hay field about 200 yards away. It was brown, bipedal, and four feet taller than a nearby fence. Rushing home to report the sighting, they learned that two relatives had passed the same field, glimpsing the creature fifteen minutes earlier.[151]

On November 21st, the day before Thanksgiving, a hunter met Bigfoot in Fayetteville's New River Gorge Preserve. As he described it to the BFRO:

I saw a very large hand appear from the side of a large poplar tree. It was palm against the tree and I saw fingers mostly. Then, to my surprise, I saw a head peek from around the large tree and two LARGE eyes affixed on a head of a creature I've never seen before...It was very cool looking, about seven feet tall. It had very dark large pupils and around the pupils its eyes were almost owl like. It had brownish blond fur and it had a visible face. It almost looked like the troll faces that you used to put on your pencils as kids.[152]

In November 2007, a Raleigh County hunter shot a deer and saw it fall, then took time to dismantle his tree stand before retrieving his kill. On arrival at the scene, he found a blood pool but no deer, and no trail leading from the site. In the BFRO's estimation, "Whatever took the deer had to have enough strength

to lift it clear of the ground and move through logging slash to exit the area."[153]

Our first report for 2008 dates from a Tuesday in winter, without further specifics. While driving through Greenbrier County near Renick (also called Falling Spring), a couple saw Bigfoot on US Route 219 at 1:30 a.m. The creature was seven to eight feet tall, with "glowing eyes." It was running north, "and its arms were long and lanky, swinging back and forth as it ran." Passing the same site again hours later, they found strands of hair bearing "a wet dog smell" stuck to a roadside fence.[154]

At 6:30 p.m. on January 21, 2008, a driver saw "something big, black, fuzzy, and walking on its hind legs" near the location of a double sighting in September, outside Shady Springs. Returning with friends, he found tracks in the snow "about the size of a men's 8½ shoe"— 10.125 inches long—separated by a stride "far wider than a human's."[155]

Two months later, on March 18th, the mother of a Raleigh County witness saw "something huge and black" standing on a hillside 200 yards from the road, while driving to a grocery in Shady Springs at 2 p.m.[156] On the same day, also near Shady Springs, a target shooter heard wood-knocking in the forest. Later, he wrote, "I can't even begin to describe how loud and forceful these sounds were."[157]

At 6:45 p.m. on March 29th, a motorist left Interstate 64 East at Exit 139, approaching the Sandstone Visitor Center (Summers County). Suddenly, he hit the brake and blurted to his fiancée, "Holy crap! I just saw Bigfoot, maybe three or four!" Doubling back to the site, his fiancée also saw the creatures, later telling the BFRO:

I spotted the group. It consisted of two large and two smaller. The larger appeared to be at least seven to eight foot tall. The smaller ones were two foot smaller. They were solid black in color...The two larger

BIGFOOT PLAYS HIDE-AND-SEEK IN YOUR GARDEN, FOR A PRICE, FROM DESIGN TOSCANO.

Credit: Author's collection

were standing uphill from the two smaller ones sitting. The group was moving back and forth. The two larger would squat then stand back up again, at least four times. I then made a howling noise and the largest one began to sway back and forth between two trees. He looked like a gorilla at the zoo holding the bars and going back and forth. I howled again and he moved downhill towards one of the smaller ones and bent over near it. There was enough light behind them for me to see arms and legs and what appeared to be a huge upper body on the largest one.[158]

In April 2008, the BFRO mounted a four-day search in Pocahontas County. Steve Willis reported wood-knocking on April 13th, while two other team members—left anonymous because they "did not want their professional reputations tainted"—found and cast a pair of tracks, one eighteen inches long, the other thirteen inches.[159]

That summer, one late afternoon, Witness X sent the GCBRO another report from Wayne County. Her daughter-in-law had seen a brown-haired creature running near her home, initially mistaking it for one of her uncle's miniature horses. She remained insistent, even after he assured her that all horses were accounted for, but Witness X believed it was Bigfoot. A second summer incident, dating from July, involved a brother of Witness X, who heard threatening growls while burning trash outdoors, then found his dog strangled in its fenced enclosure.[160]

STRANGE MONSTERS 145

On the night of August 2nd, two friends training a hunting dog near Valley Head (Randolph County) saw a pair of bluish-green eyes watching them from the forest, elevated five or six feet above ground. Curious, they approached, but the watcher fled into darkness. Returning to their truck, they saw the glowing eyes return, joined by a second pair. The witnesses departed, followed by the shiny eyes for close to half a mile.[161]

On September 12th, a mother and daughter riding an ATV near Bruceton Mills (Preston County) saw a deer stand swaying from side to side. Drawing closer, they found "a large hair covered animal," eight to nine feet tall, shaking the hunter's hideout. Since that sighting, they have noted wood-knocking sounds from the nearby forest.[162]

Later in September, two men camped in Lincoln County, near the Wayne County line, heard shrieks and tree-knocking, then found "quite a few" humanoid tracks in the forest, one thirteen inches by six.[163]

October 15th brought a teenager's report from Wayne County, near Lavalette. With a cousin, he heard an animal descending a nearby hillside, supposing it must be a deer. Just then—around 9 p.m.—a passing car's headlights revealed "something tall" standing erect, "huffing and puffing" as it turned to flee.[164]

The day after Christmas 2008, a hunter stalking deer in Tucker County's Canaan Valley National Wildlife Refuge saw the "vague silhouette" of a "large man" ninety yards distant. Peering through his rifle's scope:

I could see what appeared to be a primate-like creature standing upright and staring directly at me. It only broke its stillness to slightly move the upper portion of its body in an up and down motion. It would bend its knees as if it was going to sit down, then immediately straighten back up. This went on for what seemed to have been over a

CANAAN VALLEY NATIONAL WILDLIFE REFUGE.

minute, then the creature exited the group of trees and moved to my left (the creature's right), towards the mountain behind me.[165]

Witness X logged two more Wayne County sightings in February 2009, reported by her brothers on the twelfth and fourteenth, at their respective homes. One creature was "linebacker size," the other roughly seven feet tall, "muscular, big, but not fat." Whistling sounds accompanied the visits. One brother logged a second sighting on February 16th, describing a six-foot tall, reddish-brown biped that "screamed like a woman." Soon afterward, an unseen prowler made "a large commotion" in one brother's house as it escaped. Sometime before year's end, one of the brothers saw another creature, "gray and hairy, and very broad shouldered," walking along the highway.[166]

In April 2009, while talking to her brother on the phone, Witness X heard "what sounded like a baby crying, but also sounded like an animal," issuing from her brother's end of the line. Both attributed the sounds to Bigfoot.[167]

On the night of May 15, 2009, a girl standing outside her home near Smoot (Greenbrier County) noticed a "wet dog" smell and turned to see "a seven or eight feet tall creature that was brown, hairy, and kind of lanky" standing nearby. She ran to the house and remained there till morning, when she emerged with her parents to find footprints in their garden. The tracks were fourteen to fifteen inches long, separated by a stride of four to five feet.[168]

Eight days later, a couple riding an ATV near Shady Springs saw a black-haired biped eight to nine feet tall, near an abandoned strip mine. The driver told the BFRO, "I have totally lost interest in outdoor activities that I once loved due to this experience."[169]

On July 23rd, an anonymous witness residing near Iaeger (McDowell County) recorded the first of several purported Bigfoot encounters.

That incident involved loud screams and howls spanning forty-five minutes, emitted by an unseen creature that the witness—a longtime hunter—judged to weight 800 to 1,000 pounds. More calls woke him during August, and something slapped the side of his house in October, loud enough to rouse him from sleep. Writing to the BFRO, he recounted four undated cases: a policeman whose patrol car nearly struck "a monkey without a tail"; a neighbor who caught an eight-food biped stealing feed from her barn; two teens who saw Bigfoot emerge from "an impenetrable thicket"; and a hunter tracking a wounded deer, who lost it to some unseen scavenger.[170]

Witness X logged her next report in late summer of 2009, when something with "a huge lung capacity" roared disapproval of an impromptu front-porch guitar session. A neighbor laughed at that report—until a tree-knocking prowler lobbed a green persimmon at her head. Meanwhile, the nocturnal slaughter of family chickens and dogs continued.[171]

On September 11, 2009, a woman driving on Brushy Fork Road near Buckhannon saw Bigfoot standing at roadside, watching her pass with "animal eyes that were oddly intelligent seeming." The creature stood six to seven feet tall, with flared nostrils and pointed teeth, "like a mouth full of canine incisors."[172]

That autumn, a nephew of Witness X heard tree-knocking while he worked on an old car's motor, seeming to answer when he responded. That night, while the witness watched TV with his mother, something repeatedly struck the outer walls of their home.[173]

A similar, if less frightening story, emerged from Webster County on October 27th. That night, around 1 a.m., a "sour milk" smell pervaded the witnesses' rural home. Next, a "shadow" moved across the porch, followed by tapping on the walls, persisting for two hours. At dawn, the witnesses found "rub marks" on their walls and two footprints in the nearby forest: both measured 15½ inches long, separated by a 37½-inch stride.[174]

An anonymous Greenbrier County witness reported two sightings for 2009, one in October, the other undated. In both cases, the creature was black, stood upright at six to seven feet, and was "one foot wider" than the 260-pound witness.[175]

One night in November, around 1:30 a.m., a Wayne County resident heard loud whoops and howls near his home, followed by "a deep gurglely growl" and sounds of trees shaking.[176]

On November 28th, a hunter prowling near Cabin Creek (Kanawha County) met a smelly biped that "looked like a linebacker," standing around seven feet six inches tall.[177]

Witness X in Wayne County provides our last report for 2009, relayed from a friend. Several members of the friend's family were "sitting on their porch, about the edge of dark, just laughing and talking the way families do, when something all white, and running on two legs came charging down the hillside, screaming and breaking trees and branches as it came." The humans fled indoors and waited for the beast to leave.[178] ■

A NEW DECADE

ON MARCH 1, 2010, the daughter of a witness who saw Bigfoot near Buckhannon six months earlier logged her own sighting within a half-mile of her mother's September encounter.[179] A short time later, in Wayne County, an unnamed witness experienced his first instance of tree-knocking, protracted for twenty minutes. Other percussion serenades occurred in summer and on Labor Day (September 6).[180]

On July 4th, witness "Robbie Knight"—an admitted alias—reported branches snapping at his home near Maidsville (Monongalia County). He saw nothing, but cites an unnamed "credible source" who described the local "Beast of Bertha Hill" as white-haired, five to seven feet tall, prone to emitting "screams like a woman."[181]

Our next report comes second-hand from Fayette County, where an anonymous witness photographed one of several stone pyramids found beside the New River in August or September 2010. A friend who heard the story reported it to the GCBRO as possible evidence of Bigfoot.[182]

October 2010 brought two more reports from Witness X. One involved a prowler pounding on her brother's trailer and chasing his chickens. In the other incident, some prankster lobbed an acorn at Witness X from the forest.[183] On October 26th, Stephen Summers saw a nine-foot "ape-like" creature beside Route 19, near Crooked Run (Harrison County).[184] On October 30th, a Preston County hunter heard rock-clacking outside Pleasant Dale, near the spot where his brother found a deer mauled by some predator that "left nothing but hair."[185]

On November 1st, turkey hunters camped near Brandywine (Pendleton County) heard "a very odd howl" around midnight, followed by heavy steps circling their tent. The next morning, nearby, they found "a large pile of feces with acorns in it," which persuaded them to leave the area. Later, browsing the Internet, they matched the sound they'd heard to purported Bigfoot calls.[186]

As winter set in, two witnesses claimed a sighting of "an ape drinking water with its hands" near Blue Sulfur Springs. One observer, a former sheriff and NASA employee, wrote, "I can tell you that what I saw was not a human and not a bear. Beyond that I can't say."[187]

Greenbrier County produced its next sighting on January 5, 2011. A driver and his adult son saw the creature on Interstate 64, "running like a sprinter runs," and swerved to avoid collision. It was covered in long, dark brown hair and tall enough that its shoulder matched the height of a cradle on a logging truck parked at roadside.[188]

Twelve days later, Witness X reported another Bigfoot-related "commotion" in Wayne County, at her brother's home. He saw no creature, but his dogs went berserk overnight, and dawn's light revealed strange drag marks in the yard, still unexplained. On January 30th, familiar tree-knocking resumed at Witness X's home.[189]

On May 5, 2011, Witness X's brother reported "big and loud" howls at his home, winding down to a sinister "werewolf" growl. Three weeks later, on May 26th, the "wailing yells" resumed, reminding him of supposed Bigfoot vocalizations recorded online. More disturbing cries were heard on July 15th and 17th, then again in August. Around the same time as the last report, Witness X's niece glimpsed a hairy biped prowling near her home. It was "a 'dingy' or dirty white, almost sandy in color," and snarled at sight of her.[190]

On August 31, 2011, Bigfoot researchers Russ Jones and Darren Pevarnik recorded eerie nocturnal cries in Pendleton County and posted the sound byte on YouTube.[191] September 8th brought two reported sightings from the son of a West Virginia Bigfoot Research Association member: one incident, on September 7th, involved frightening noises in the forest; the other, occurring "about a month ago," included "red eyeshine from the weeds." Neither account gave a location for the incidents.[192]

In late November, Ohio residents Terri Bessler and Crystal Krieger saw Bigfoot in West Virginia, while driving to North Carolina. Bessler said, "It was huge, there is no way it was a person." Krieger added, "If it was a real person, it was the biggest person in the world. And where would they be going? There is nothing up there but woods." Again, sadly, the location remains undisclosed.[193]

Around the same time, a hunter seeking deer in Lewis County met a black biped six to seven feet tall, with dark red eyes. Frightened, he fired four shots from a .30-caliber M1 carbine, whereupon the beast uttered "an unearthly scream" and fled. The shooter tried to follow, but he found no blood trail.[194]

Sightings lagged in 2012. Four of the year's six reports are restricted to sounds associated with Bigfoot: screams near Wildell on April 26th and 27th; wood-knocking near Franklin (Pendleton County) on May 19th; rock-clacking and heavy footsteps on Shavers Mountain (Pocahontas County) in June; and "possible vocals" near Sugar Grove (Pendleton County) on August 30th.[195]

The year's first sighting occurred on November 19th, near Franklin. Two hunters heard a whooping cry "so loud it almost sounded as if it came from an amplifier," but proceeded with their quest. After lunch, while mounting a tree stand, one heard "a very angry growl and what sounded like two rocks being smashed together violently." Turning, he saw "a large black/dark brown head and shoulders quickly duck behind a boulder," prompting him to flee at top speed.[196]

On December 28th, another pair of hunters—Levi Byers and Dustin Ostrowski—met Bigfoot near Williamstown (Wood County). Ostrowski shot a doe, and while pursuing it, encountered an eight-foot-tall biped with "muscle, a lot of it."[197]

Our first Bigfoot report of 2013 dates from January, when three teenagers working on a school project allegedly "captured images of

A VIEW FROM SHAVERS MOUNTAIN.

Sasquatch in a West Virginia forest and collected its hair samples." One youth described the creature to police as "very large and hunched." That report drew television's *Finding Bigfoot* team to search in vain along the 'Greenbrier River.[198]

Eight months passed before the next sighting, in August. A woman visiting a lodge in Tucker County saw a "huge" biped "running in big leaping strides" alongside the highway. She described its hair as "an orangey brown color a little darker than a deer." A follow-up investigation by the West Virginia Bigfoot Investigations Group found "tracks, bent over trees, scratches on trees, believed to be too high to be done by bears, and a possible teepee structure."[199]

On August 14th, at Bear Haven Campground near Elkins, campers heard Bigfoot-style whooping around 3 a.m.[200] The year's last incident, undated, occurred in Boone County, where a couple saw an apelike creature on their property. According to that report:

...something about four feet in height jumped off a wall to the left of our back yard...It made two jumps in our back yard (approx. twenty-foot jumps) and landed on a chain-linked fence and steadied it self with its right hand on a branch. It then jumped to the corner of the chain-linked fence (approx. sixteen feet) and jumped off. It then made two to three more jumps past our neighbors house and was gone.[201] ■

>> DATES UNKNOWN

WEST VIRGINIA'S BIGFOOT file includes fourteen incidents reported without years, much less specific dates, attached. I have arranged them alphabetically, by county, where that basic information was provided.

From Bridgeport (Harrison County) comes the tale of a farmer who shot a strange creature seen leaping from tree to tree. According to the story:

> It had long grayish, brown hair and was about five feet tall. Its hands were human like and its feet was more hand like then anything. I told my friend he was crazy so he decided to prove it to me. He took me to the old barn and there it was. The old man had nailed its carcass to the wall. I was shocked it was built a lot like a human had hair six or seven inches long on it. It had very large sharp teeth and resembled some kind of monkey looking creature.[202]

Reports of the Morgan Ridge Monster in Fairmont (Marion County) begin with the O'Dell family, poor farmers who lost several sheep to a hulking bipedal predator, before they pursued and shot it. While never recovered, the beast ceased to trouble them after the shooting.[203]

A later report from Marion County describes a hunter's experience on Guyan Creek Road, near Glenwood. While climbing the hill, he says, "a large limb hit me in the back and a roar or scream that I can't describe was directed toward me."[204]

Another hunter, in Mingo County, first smelled "some very dank odor (such as a wet dog but stronger)," then saw an eight-foot

Credit: Author's collection.

GUYAN CREEK ROAD, NEAR GLENWOOD.

biped covered in brownish orange hair, descending the hillside "way too easy to be a man." The hunter fled.[205]

On Baker Ridge (Monongalia County), a house-sitting college student reported seeing "a monster behaving suspiciously like a juvenile Bigfoot." It was white, about five feet tall, with red eyes and "hair sticking out all over its head, messy and un-groomed." It slapped at windows, jiggled doors, and generally made a pest of itself before leaving.[206]

Pocahontas County offers four undated sightings, three from a single anonymous witness. He described the garden-raiding biped as a "human shaped creature standing over fifteen feet [tall] with red shining eyes that were several inches if not a foot apart." It was covered in "black nappy matted hair that was faded to brown on the arms...The arms were huge and seemed to touch the ground." In flight, the thing ran on all fours and "covered one hundred yards in a second or two." The other witness met a whistling Bigfoot at a beaver pond, emitting a "musky mildew dog crap smell."[207]

Witness X provides one last tale from Wayne County, in which she heard heavy footsteps crossing her roof one night. Relatives, called to investigate, found a pile of feces on the roof in "a cinnamon roll shape, as large as a dinner plate."[208]

E-mail correspondent "Canadian David" writes from Boaz (Wood County), describing multiple childhood encounters with "a large black furry beast that stands about seven feet tall when on its hind legs, [with] sharp teeth that goes after weaker feed." The creature never threatened him, but made two appearances at David's home after nightfall.[209]

Finally, we have a report filed by "Brittany and Dylan," with no date or county included. The friends, aged eight and twelve, first found a large humanoid footprint, then saw a red-eyed, seven-foot-tall creature "sitting like a frog would, staring at us." On another woodland excursion, friend "Franky" was seized by some unknown prowler and hurled through the air, left "scratched all up down his leg."[210] ∎

CHAPTER 9

THE
GREAT
UNKNOWN

Our survey of West Virginia cryptids, inevitably, leaves us with some dangling loose ends. The realm of "monsters" is so diverse, so bizarre, that some creatures are bound to fall outside the broad categories established by Chapters 1 through 8. Some gathered here, in our overflow menagerie, may vaguely resemble phantom felines, devil dogs, or hulking apemen, but each has some unique—and sometimes terrifying—aspect to distinguish it. We shall review these cases chronologically, insofar as possible, and see where the final lap of our strange journey leads. ■

GRAFTON, WEST VIRGINIA, REPUTED HOME OF AN ELUSIVE MONSTER.

>> "HALF EATEN UP"

Credit: Library of Congress

FUTURE PRESIDENT THOMAS JEFFERSON REPORTED A MYSTERIOUS PREDATOR AT LARGE IN 1799.

IN HIS FEBRUARY 1797 address to the American Philosophical Society, Vice President Thomas Jefferson related the following tale of a ferocious predator at large in the region that would later become West Virginia.

A person of the name of Draper had gone in the year 1770 to hunt on the Kanhawa

[sic]. He had turned his horse loose with a bell on, and had not yet got out of hearing when his attention was recalled by the rapid ringing of the bell. Suspecting that Indians might be attempting to take off his horse he immediately returned to him, but before he arrived he was half eaten up. His dog scenting the trace of a wild beast, he followed him on it, and soon came in sight of an animal of such enormous size, that tho [sic] one of our most daring hunters, and best marksmen he withdrew instantly and as silently as possible, checking and bringing off his dog. He could recollect no more of the animal than his terrific bulk and that his general outlines were those of the Cat kind. He was familiar with our animal miscalled the panther, with our wolves and wild beasts generally and would not have mistaken nor shrunk from them.[1]

Whatever the creature was, a relict cave lion or something even more formidable, it survived that engagement to hunt another day. ∎

>> AN APPALACHIAN PEGASUS

ON JULY 8, 1878, the *New York Times* reprinted a telegram sent from Parkersburg, West Virginia, to the *Cincinnati Sentinel*. It read:

An optical illusion or mirage was seen by three or four farmers a few miles from this city a few days since, the appearance of which no one is able philosophically to

FLYING HORSES ARE ICONIC FIGURES DATING FROM GRECO-ROMAN MYTHOLOGY.

account for. The facts are these: A gentleman, while plowing in a field with several others, about 7 p.m., happened to glance toward the sky, which was cloudless, and saw apparently, about half a mile off in a westerly direction, an opaque substance, resembling a white horse, with head, neck, limbs, and tail clearly defined, swimming in the clear atmosphere. It appeared to be moving its limbs as if engaged in swimming, moving its head from side to side, always ascending at an angle of about 45°. He rubbed his eyes to convince himself that he was not dreaming, and looked again; but there it still was, still apparently swimming and ascending in ether. He called to the men, about 100 yards off, and told them to look up, and tell him what they saw. They declared they saw a white horse swimming in the sky, and were badly frightened. Our informant, neither superstitious nor nervous, sat down and watched the phantasm, (if we may so call it) until it disappeared in space, always going in the same direction, and moving in the same manner. No one can account for the mirage, or illusion, except upon the uneven state of the atmosphere. Illusions of a different appearance have been seen at different times, in the same vicinity, frightening the superstitious and laughed at by the skeptical.[2]

The flying—or "swimming"—horse in this case hardly qualifies as monstrous, and indeed was probably some kind of optical illusion as suggested in the telegram. Why Parkersburg should suddenly be subject to such sightings, with or without an "uneven state of the atmosphere," remains unexplained. Some, including the late John Keel, might suggest that it reinforces West Virginia's status as a "window" for mysterious phenomena, illusory or otherwise. ∎

>> "A PRETTY MYSTICAL PLACE"

COULD THE KILLER BEAST OF GAULEY MARSH HAVE BEEN A PUFF ADDER?

Credit: US Fish & Wildlife Service

IN 1882, first a dog, then a horse, were found dead on the fringes of Gauley Marsh, in Pocahontas County. In each case, the victims were unmarked beyond a pair of wounds resembling widely spaced fang marks, thus ruling out attack by known carnivorous mammals. At the same time, the space between punctures—three and one-quarter inches—eliminated West Virginia's only venomous snakes, the timber rattler and the northern copperhead (*Agkistrodon contortrix*), as potential culprits. Hunters brought a hound to track the killer, and while the dog appeared to catch a scent, it refused to give chase.

Frustrated on that front, locals focused their suspicion next on newcomer James Brooden, who had settled in the swamp. He had examined the dead horse's wounds and suggested it was bitten by some deadly unknown snake. The horse's owner, Jonas

Heeb, suspected Brooden of involvement in that case—and when Heeb died in turn near the marsh, with identical puncture wounds on his wrist or throat (reports differ), Brooden was charged with his murder.

The "evidence" against him was an arrowhead, one of many he possessed, that seemed to match Heeb's wounds. Brooden claimed he used the arrowheads for hunting, shunning firearms, and while no trace of any poison was discovered at his camp which might have caused Heeb's death, the murder trial proceeded, climaxed by a field trip to the site where Brooden and Heeb were last seen quarreling. There, near a wall at one edge of the swamp, the judge, jurors and lawyers found a hired man burning logs and trash, oblivious to their proceedings.

While the prosecution and defense were bent on scoring points, a "low humming wail" distracted them, coming from the far side of the wall. Suddenly, a beast appeared, described as having "a club-like body four feet long. It possessed a large heart-shaped head, broader than a hand. It was colored as to disguise its presence in nature."[3]

Brooden sprang into action, grabbing the hired man's pitchfork to skewer the creature and fling it onto the nearby fire, where it wriggled and died. Pulled from the flames when it was clearly dead, the creature was examined cautiously. Those present peered into its mouth and "teeth were found that matched the known wounds. Poison sacs were seen there also containing a straw-colored venom."[4]

Brooden's murder charge was dismissed on the spot, and he wisely left the county. Folklorist G. D. McNeil, writing in 1940, summarized local opinions of the creature.

Some explained that the Marsh was but a remnant of a greater marsh which in another age had harbored many monsters now extinct; and, it was argued, the peculiar snake-like thing was the lone survivor of a dreaded species that had infested the big marsh thousands of years ago. Others maintained that the creature was no more than a monstrous deformity born from a mating of rattlesnakes.[5]

We are hampered, in attempting to identify the creature, by a dearth of physical description. Did the beast have legs? Did it have scales? There is no reason to believe a "lone survivor" of some ancient species, so aggressive in its final days, went undiscovered from the county's settlement, in the 1750s, until 1882. A "monstrous mutation" is always possible, but there may be another explanation, as well.

Our brief description of the Gauley Marsh creature—snake-like, with a "club-like" body, broad "heart-shaped" (i.e., triangular) head with fangs and venom sacs, camouflage

coloration—matches in all respects a stout-bodied viper, though not one of a domestic breed. Two species that immediately match the general description are the puff adder (*Bitis arietans*) and Gabon viper (*B. gabonica*), both native to Africa, with the puff adder's range including the southern Arabian Peninsula.

Puff adders kill more humans each year than any other venomous snake in Africa. The largest specimen on record measured six feet, three inches long, with a girth of sixteen inches, "club-like" enough with the body extended. Its color pattern varies geographically, with the ground-color ranging from straw yellow to reddish brown, overlaid with a pattern of dark brown to black bands extending from the neck to the tail.

Gabon vipers, native to eighteen countries in Central and West Africa, are the continent's heaviest venomous snakes, holding a record confirmed weight of twenty-five pounds with an empty stomach. That specimen, caught in 1973, measured five feet, nine inches in length. Girths of 14.65 inches are confirmed, and Gabon vipers pack the longest fangs of any known venomous snake, measuring up to 2.2 inches. The standard color pattern consists of pale sub-rectangular blotches running down the center of the back, interspersed with dark, yellow-edged hourglass markings. Rhomboidal shapes mark the flanks, ranging from tan to brown, the overall pattern providing excellent forest floor camouflage.

Neither viper can produce a "low humming wail"—nor can any other snake, since they lack vocal cords—but puff adders derive their name from the loud hissing sounds they emit when disturbed. As to how either species might have made the trip from Africa to West Virginia in the nineteenth century, we may only speculate. A long shot solution perhaps, but still more logical than a lone prehistoric survivor inhabiting Gauley Marsh for generations, unnoticed.

Credit: US Fish & Wildlife Service

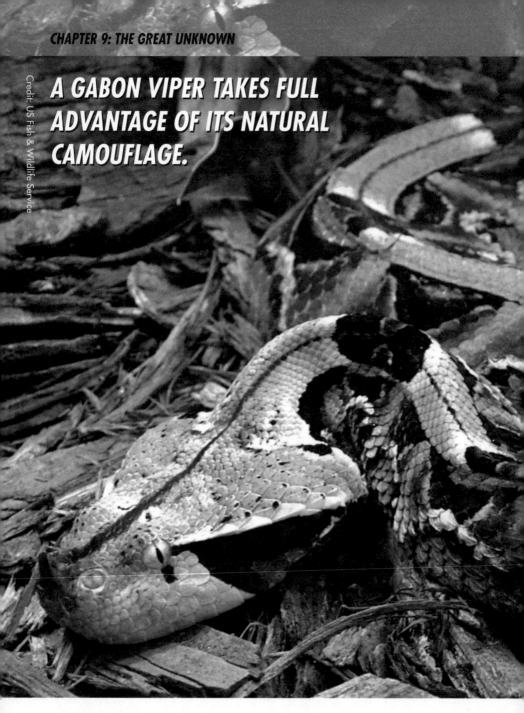

A GABON VIPER TAKES FULL ADVANTAGE OF ITS NATURAL CAMOUFLAGE.

Credit: US Fish & Wildlife Service

In October 2012, the Pocahontas County Opera House presented a play based on the Brooden murder trial, performed outdoors on the boardwalk of the Cranberry Glades Botanical Area. Director Emily Newton fairly summarized the history of Gauley Marsh, telling reporters, "We live in a pretty mystical place. You don't actually know what is around every corner of every trail."[6] ■

STREAKING IN ELKHORN

ON NOVEMBER 10, 1895, the *Columbus* (Indiana) *Daily Times* carried the following brief report:

> *Bluefield, W. Va., Nov. 9—A party of hunters who were roaming the woods on Elkhorn [McDowell County] saw a man ascending a rocky height completely naked. The hunters surrounded the fellow and made an attempt to capture him, but as soon as he saw the men he yelled and ran to the top of the hill. He is not sought for.*[7]

If local authorities were not concerned about the woodland streaker, why are we? Renowned UFO researcher Albert Rosales includes this report in his huge database of some 4,000 "humanoid cases" collected online.[8] While most of those entries describe creatures seen with unidentified flying objects, Rosales also includes Mothman sightings, reports of Bigfoot-type bipeds, and other anomalous entities. The Elkhorn nudist was clearly "humanoid"—as in *human*—but nothing suggests extraterrestrial origin. He was, in all likelihood, a mentally unbalanced hermit. ■

AN OGDEN ODDITY

ROSALES STRIKES CLOSER to the mark with a report from April 21, 1897. The event occurred near Ogden (Wood County), misspelled "Ogdin" in the online summary that reads:

> *A witness claimed he saw a well-lit object land nearby. The man swore the eight creatures aboard the craft were between eleven and twelve feet tall, with disproportionately large heads. According to the witness, the creatures told him they were exploring the planet. They ate small pills and "drank air" before their ship took off after an hour-long stay.*[9]

Unfortunately, this early report of a supposed UFO landing in West Virginia offers no further details. Rosales cites a book by Fortean author Philip L. Rife as his source for the story—and the "Ogdin" misspelling—but Rife's garbled reference notes cite his source as the *British Daily Whig*, published on November 15, 1865. With that impossibility in mind, we note that an adjacent reference note cites the *Parsons Advocate* of April 23, 1897, published in Tucker County.[10] The trail ends there, as contact with the *Advocate* produced no copy of the article or any further information. ■

>> FIRECO'S BRAIN-EATER

FIRECO IS AN unincorporated town in Raleigh County's Winding Gulf Coalfield, named for the heat produced by coal from its mines. On May 11, 1934, Beckley's *Raleigh Register* published the following account of a mysterious predator at large.

> From Fireco come reports of a strange creature that, appearing in that vicinity three weeks ago, has slain hogs and dogs, carried away chickens, and frightened people by violent antics.
>
> Henry Beard, eighth grade Sloco student, and the Reverend Artie Ward, colored minister, profess to have seen the creature, and their combined meager description indicate[s] only that it is "about two feet tall," has "yellowish gray hair," and "runs like the wind."
>
> Three dogs owned by Floyd Terry, of Fireco, chased the strange varmint into an old drift-mouth. Presently two dogs came running forth as if possessed; the third dog remained behind, its head snatched off.
>
> Upon its first appearance three weeks ago, the animal, if animal it be, attacked three hogs, tore off their heads, ate the brains and then decamped, leaving the carcasses behind. Shortly thereafter it was reported elsewhere in the community, and this time two hogs were left separated from their heads and brains.

> The creature, according to information, is fond of hog brains.
>
> Last Wednesday night the Reverend Artie Ward heard a commotion among his chickens. He arrived at the chicken-yard fence barely in time to see a strange, yellowish-gray-haired animal clear the six-foot fence at a leap and disappear, leaving some of the hair clinging to the fence.
>
> As a result of these depredations, residents of the community are frightened and their dogs are so terrified that they remain in their owners' yards and howl mournfully.
>
> Thus far nobody has been found who knows exactly what the dog-killing, hog-head-snatching creature is, nor is there any accurate description of him. Residents of the Fireco vicinity speak speculatively of wolves, panthers, and it has been suggested that some unnatural hybrid has resulted from an unusual association of animal life.[11]

The mauler's vague description, as to size and color, generally matches a coyote, but that canid is not known for beheading its prey or dining primarily on brains. Nor are timber wolves, assuming any managed to survive their species' official extirpation in 1900. Whatever the Fireco brain-eater was, it apparently vanished from Raleigh County as suddenly and mysteriously as it had come. ∎

>> THE BLUE DEVIL

WEBSTER COUNTY SPAWNED A MONSTER of its own in autumn 1939, described as a "horse-faced blue devil with a yell like a banshee."[12] Residents of the Diana-Grassy Creek district set out bear traps for the creature, in vain, while hunters scoured the forest. By mid-December the prowler had expanded its range to include Jumbo and Webster Springs, where locals amended prior statements to describe a "dog-faced blue devil."[13]

All agreed that the creature had a taste for livestock, mauling sheep and cattle, also killing John Clevenger's pricey hunting dog at Jumbo. Two anonymous "bear hunters from New York City" arrived to track the beast with hounds, but "after a short time [the dogs] came slinking back, refusing to trail the scent any longer."[14]

Glen Fisher, meanwhile, claimed to have killed the creature in late November. As detailed in the *Charleston Daily Mail* on December 13th, "He said he shot some kind of an animal two weeks ago and saw it jump up in the air as the bullet struck. He said he waited until morning to see what he had shot, but that the animal disappeared. Since then, he said, the blue devil has not been seen in the Grassy Creek section."[15]

On Christmas Eve, with tongue firmly planted in cheek, the Clarksburg *Telegram*'s editor suggested that the Blue Devil might be "an overgrown relation of the small animal known as the mole." While granting that moles cannot shriek like banshees, he noted that they rank among the most voracious animals on Earth, one West Virginia specimen having been observed to eat 132 percent of its own body weight within twenty-four hours.[16]

On that jocular note, the Blue Devil took leave of Webster County, perhaps moving on to neighboring Randolph. There, in January 1940, "some strange critter" began raiding sheep herds around Gauley Mountain, on the Randolph-Pocahontas County line. The *Charleston Gazette* suspected a "panther" at work, but veteran ranchers denied any cat, dog, or bear was to blame for their losses.[17]

Wayne Stalnaker, with the Conservation Commission's law enforcement department, viewed the creature's tracks and agreed with the ranchers. While noting Stalnaker's "broad knowledge of the woods and their inhabitants," praising his "impeccable veracity," the *Gazette* still mused, "We'd like some student of the wilds to take a look at them tracks."[18]

Apparently, none did—nor were the tracks ever described in print. After its last hurrah at Gauley Mountain, the Blue Devil vanished and was seen no more. ∎

THE GRAFTON MONSTER

TWO DECADES AFTER the Blue Devil vanished, in June 1964, a very different creature made its first appearance on Riverside Drive, in Grafton. The first witness was Robert Cockrell, a reporter for the Grafton *Sentinel*. Cockrell published stories on the creature and the panic it inspired, but Mark Hall later claimed that "the story was so censored by the paper's editor that it was barely recognizable."[19]

Hall knew that much because Cockrell told the full story to author Gray Barker, who in turn left his files to the Clarksburg-Harrison Public Library at his death, in 1984. As Cockrell described the events to Barker:

On the night of June 16th at 11 p.m. I was on my way home and averaging 50 m.p.h. I know the road well, the night was clear. I was not overly tired or exhausted nor was I under any emotional stress. As I was coming down the road I was negotiating a wide curve. As I came out of the curve I looked down the mile-long straight stretch ahead. As I glanced up, my high beams

GRAFTON, WEST VIRGINIA, REPUTED HOME OF AN ELUSIVE MONSTER.

picked up a huge white obstruction on the right side of the road standing between the road and the river bank on a cleared off section of grass.

After glimpsing the Thing, I speeded up to get off that road as soon as possible. My impressions of the beast were: It was between seven and nine feet tall, it was approximately four feet wide, and has a seal like skin or covering which had a sheen to it. It had no discernible head and did not move as I passed by. This is the only accurate description I can give since I was deeply frightened by the sight.[20]

Cockrell conquered his fear and returned to the site with two friends, finding some flattened brush but no visible tracks. Searching the riverside for over an hour, the three men

heard a "low whistling sound" at one point, but could not identify its source.[21]

After his first story ran in the *Sentinel*, teenagers joined in the monster hunt, briefly thronging Riverside Drive with their hotrods and making a nuisance of themselves until authorities intervened. The events are largely forgotten today, and researcher Kurt McCoy, writing in April 2007, reported that Cockrell—still living at that time—refused to answer his letters and phone calls.[22]

Cockrell's scanty description of the Grafton Monster evokes images of Sheepsquatch, until we read of the creature's sleek "seal like skin" and its lack of a visible head. Though white, it seems not to be the wooly, horned monstrosity we met in Chapter 5. And what that leaves, in terms of likely candidates, is anybody's guess. ■

NEW HAVEN'S HEART-SNATCHER

FIVE YEARS AFTER the Grafton flap, one April morning in 1969, Ernest Adkins found his eleven-week-old beagle puppy dead in the yard of his farmhouse at New Haven, ten miles northeast of Point Pleasant. As Adkins described the grim scene to John Keel, "There was no evidence that the dog had died in a fight. But there was a large, very neat hole in its side, and the animal's heart was lying outside the body. It looked as if something chewed it out. There were no other marks on the body."[23]

No predator known to science kills in that manner, or would logically leave heart and carcass uneaten. The incident's timing and proximity to Point Pleasant stirred up memories of Mothman, but aside from one speculative account of Mothman snatching a dead dog at roadside, nothing connects that flying apparition to any acts of predation. The beagle's death remains an unsolved mystery. ∎

THE INTIMIDATOR

WHILE RESIDENTS OF OCEANA were dodging large silver-blue birds in August 1978 (see Chapter 4), they also had to contend with another cryptid, dubbed the "Oceana Intimidator" by reporter Steve Williams of Charleston's *Daily News*. Unlike the feathered phantom, this one was humanoid in form, but with astounding capabilities—and an apparent taste for chicken bones.

Police officer Bill Pritt met the Intimidator on Tuesday night, August 8th, observed by neighbor Edward Cook as Cook peered from a window of his home on Clear Fork Street. "I saw what I thought was a man," Pritt told Williams, "about six and a half feet tall." He estimated the figure's weight at 200 to 300 pounds, seen in profile beneath a streetlight.[24]

Police Chief Raymond Walker arrived seconds later, turning the encounter from suspicious to downright weird. "As soon as the headlights hit it," Britt said, "it turned its back to me." The figure "hunkered down," then leaped over a fifteen-foot-wide creek bed, landing on the opposite bank. Pritt and Walker both fired their pistols toward the fleeing prowler, but "not directly at it" as described by Cook.[25]

Steve Williams hyped the story for all it was worth, writing on August 28th: "There's a common criminal loose in this Wyoming County community. To date he faces charges for only one crime—intimidation. It's possible the culprit may be linked to the theft of a number of chicken bones left stacked on a city resident's porch, police report. As far as police can surmise, the accused has not harmed anyone."[26]

Nor would he—or it—despite the panic successive sightings inspired. At dawn on August 9, a fifteen-man posse discovered sixteen-inch "pawprints" at the shooting scene, trailing them "along the creek bank and railroad tracks and then up over the mountain, disappearing at the top." Bill Pritt complained that dogs were useless in the hunt. "When that thing hollered you couldn't find a dog in town nowhere," he said, "so I've been watching the dogs. If the dogs disappear, I know that bastard's back."[27]

Pritt's effort was halfhearted, though. "I'm looking, hoping I don't see it," he told Williams, "cause it's something I definitely don't want to see any more."[28]

Others had seen the Intimidator, however, and were glad to talk about it. One Wyoming County witness claimed a sighting from the previous winter. A woman in Nicholas County wrote to Chief Walker, saying, "We've had a thousand reports." Officer Pritt, for his part, was pleased when other local witnesses came forward. "I ain't taking too much ribbing now," he said, "cause too many other people say they have seen it besides me. I've never believed in that kind of thing myself, but now this thing has made a believer out of me."[29]

As to what "kind of thing" it was—or where it went, after receiving so much publicity—we have no clue today. ∎

>> "SHAKING LIKE DON KNOTTS"

IN JULY 2004, e-mail correspondent Brian Martin shared a story from his Pocahontas County childhood, occurring in late spring or early summer of 1979. Martin's mother was driving her three sons home to Neola one night, when their pickup truck threw its fan belt, overheated, and died twelve miles north of town. Left afoot, they had covered a half-mile when "something let out a blood curdling scream less than a hundred feet away."[30] Older brother Shawn produced a flashlight, but its beam revealed only thick brush and woods on each side of the road.

The family moved on, badly frightened, while the screaming creature followed. Martin recalls The animal would always remain just out of the range of the light beam. We never saw it, but it was well aware of us and our position at all times.

We continued walking towards home, with this creature letting out a blood curdling scream at least every ninety seconds or so. It was systematically circling our position, so as to confuse us into thinking we were totally surrounded by numerous animals. I still believe it was only one.[31]

Closer to home, the beast scaled a roadside ore pile and "let out one last roar as we walked past. My brother Shawn pointed the light in the direction of the noise. I noticed at that time he was shaking like [comic actor] Don Knotts."[32] By then, Martin could hear his dogs barking nearby and called them to him, putting the still unseen prowler to flight. His mother heard it fleeing up a nearby hollow, toward an abandoned cabin and out of their lives forever. ∎

>> WILD THING

CODY MILLS POSTED our next tale online in April 2013, relating an experience shared by two of his uncles and a companion in the Kyawiley region of Wayne County, an area "so rural, the roads cannot be seen on maps and the road disappears into the creek and

EAST LYNN LAKE, IN WAYNE COUNTY.

heads into the forest near the East Lynn Lake."[33] On this occasion, sometime in the 1980s, the brothers and their friend repaired to a wilderness cabin built the previous year, using it as their base for deer hunting.

At 1 a.m. on their third night at the cabin, a large creature roused them from sleep with unusual sounds, including "a deep slow breathing."[34] It circled the cabin, then departed—but returned at the same time the following night. On its second visit, the creature stepped onto the cabin's front porch, moving with a measured stride that made the frightened men inside surmise that it was walking on two legs. Was it a man, perhaps, intent on doing harm?

After multiple shouted warnings, one hunter emptied his gun through the cabin's window, followed by sounds of the night-prowler fleeing. Mills described what happened next.

Using coon lights, they followed the blood trail through the brush and cattail by the lake's edge and then up a mountain. When they reached the top of the mountain, they were surprised to find an old building, possibly a schoolhouse or church left behind from when the old mining town of East Lynn was booming, before they flooded the town and created East Lynn Lake.

The blood trail led into a large hole on the side of the building. It was barely daylight now and they could see just enough to get the boards off the door to get inside the building. What they found was very peculiar and sends a lot of questions through my mind. Toward the back of the building the boards were torn from the structure and the dirt from the ground was visible. There was an imprint in the ground approximately seven feet long. The imprint, my uncle said, reminded him of what you'd see when you look at a typical doghouse when a dog digs him a spot to sleep. An indention in the earth with no grass and nearly a foot deep. Around this large hole were animal bones, piled up. The blood trail was lost. Just as soon as they had made this discovery, it began to rain. My uncle, his brother, and friend were terrified.[35]

The trio cut short their safari, and Mills's uncle had nearly forgotten the incident when he returned for another Kyawiley hunting expedition three years later. Stalking alone on that occasion, he met a neighboring landowner who inquired about any prowlers seen in the vicinity. Several of the neighbor's horses had been killed, found with "their throat from their jawbone to their breastplate removed by some type of animal or person."[36] A week after that unsettling conversation, the hunter started for home, driving along a gravel road beside his neighbor's property. Mills writes:

As he passed the old man's horse pasture, he noticed a horse at the fence-line which was panicking and letting out a horrible screech. He stopped his jeep and got out. Just then, he said as soon as he shut the door to his jeep, a creature jumped from off the fence-line and cleared the road in a single jump. It passed the lights of his jeep, so he got a clear look at its backside. He said it was about six feet tall with sharp claws and it was hairy with grayish fur. It wasn't humanlike, like a description of Bigfoot, but it was no coyote or other predator. This creature was on two legs.[37]

The road measured fifteen feet wide, reminding us of the leap made by Oceana's Intimidator some years earlier, but otherwise the vague descriptions do not match. Whatever the "Kyawiley Wildthing" was, we have no further reports of eyewitness encounters. ■

>> SLIP HILL

WITNESS "LINDA" OFFERS our next story, harking back to a late night in 2001, when she and her husband were homeward bound on a road called Slip Hill, near Parsons.

We were almost to the end of it and up ahead the lights of our truck shone on two red eyes. I thought I was seeing things. I asked my husband, "What was that?" and he said, "I don't know, but it has red eyes." When we got up to the place where we saw it, we stopped. My husband who was driving rolled down his window and was looking down over the hill, but could not see anything. The whole time we were setting there, I was getting a bad feeling coming over me. I kept asking him to please go. I was really scared. I just kept imagining it jumping up and grabbing him. I could feel that is what it was going to do. Finally, I did get him to get going. He was very scared as well. I must say my husband is not one to scare very easy and no animal has ever made him feel the way he did that night.[38]

Eyeshine is a visual effect produced by the *tapetum lucidum* ("bright tapestry" in Latin), a layer of reflective tissue found immediately behind the retina in many vertebrates, increasing the light available to the eye's photoreceptors and thereby improving night vision. Green eyeshine is common in cats, dogs and raccoons, while horses often display blue eyeshine, and red eyeshine is seen most often in coyotes, opossums, rodents and birds. Animals with heterochromia—two different-colored eyes, may also display red eyeshine from a blue eye, while showing yellow or green eyeshine from the other. That said, without an estimate of size for the Slip Hill creature, speculation as to its identity is pointless. ∎

A CAT WITH HETEROCHROMIA DISPLAYS VARIANT EYESHINE.

>> FOUR-TOES IN CABELL COUNTY

E-MAIL CORRESPONDENT ROBIN SIMMS, a resident of Milton, posted an account of strange footprints found by her children near their home, in September 2005. The first print was found in summer of 2002, at a nearby creek bed. She wrote:

It was about the size of a woman's seven or eight [9¼ to 9½ inches long]. It had three toes pointing forward and one toe at the side, sort of like where your thumb is positioned on your hand. We could clearly see the claws at the end of each toe in the mud. It looked to be made from something that walked on two legs. From what we could tell, it took a step from a rocky road, down into the mud, then on

into the water. We figured that is the reason only one footprint could be seen.[39]

Three years later, in mid-September 2005, Robin's children found "this very same footprint...way back in the hills." Her e-mail closed with the ominous observation, "Whatever it is is still around."[40]

Mention of a protruding thumb-like toe reminds us of an ape's or monkey's feet, but all normal primates possess five toes with toenails, in lieu of claws. Tracks left by cats, dogs and rabbits may display four toes, but none have an opposed toe as described by Mills, much less nine-inch-long feet. Whatever left the isolated tracks near Milton may be "still around." It certainly is unidentified. ∎

>> CEMETERY SCREAMS

AT MIDNIGHT ON JUNE 24, 2003, e-mail correspondent "Aaron R." embarked on his evening constitutional at Fort Ashby (Mineral County), planning to complete forty laps of Frankfort Cemetery, east of town on Cemetery Road. That routine normally consumed two hours, but on this occasion he was interrupted at 1:45 a.m., by screams from the nearby woods that "sounded like a female getting raped or murdered." Despite his instant fear, Aaron moved toward the source of those intimidating sounds.

I went closer to the trees to help, but it was not human and it was not hurt. It ran past me at a high rate of speed and it turned back and looked at me for four seconds. It was pure white, had pointy teeth, and had feet of a horse. It ran off, up the remote

mountain. You could even hear it scream again from up there.[41]

In retrospect, Aaron recalled "a few other times I heard noises like huge snaps of wood breaking in the woods and small hisses from the woods, but at the time I figured deer and weak tree limbs. The trees are old as it is, but now I wonder."[42]

We may question whether Aaron, in the circumstances—frightened in the dark, a snarling apparition running past him at top speed—was accurate in his description of the creature's feet and teeth. Fangs probably impressed him more than hooves, but in the absence of more evidence, who knows? The beast that he describes was clearly not a cougar, which might otherwise have been a screamer candidate. As matters stand, the thing he saw resembles nothing known to science. ∎

FRANKFORT CEMETERY IN FORT ASHBY.

> BLUEFIELD'S GARGOYLE

ANOTHER E-MAIL CORRESPONDENT, "Robert S.," provides our next case of a strange cryptid at large. Posted online in April 2004, the story relates an event from his childhood, occurring soon after his family moved to Bluefield (Mercer County), occupying a house on Longview Avenue. One afternoon, while playing with Matchbox cars near a neighbor's tall hedge, Robert had a frightening experience.

I was sitting there in broad sunny daylight when all of a sudden I saw rustling in the hedges. I looked over and out popped what I can only put into words as a gargoyle! It looked at me with solid, pointed black eyes. It had frog-green skin. Its face looked like a frog except it had teeth and ears that I'll never forget for the rest of my life. Its ears flexed outward like two big green gloves on the side of its head, like the king that the gargoyles in statues has [sic]. Its body was shaped like a bulldog and its webbed feet turned inward as it walked. Once it saw me, it paused and opened its mouth wide open and hissed. He held it wide open as if to taste the air. I was so scared that I was completely paralyzed. I tried to cry for help, but nothing came out. And

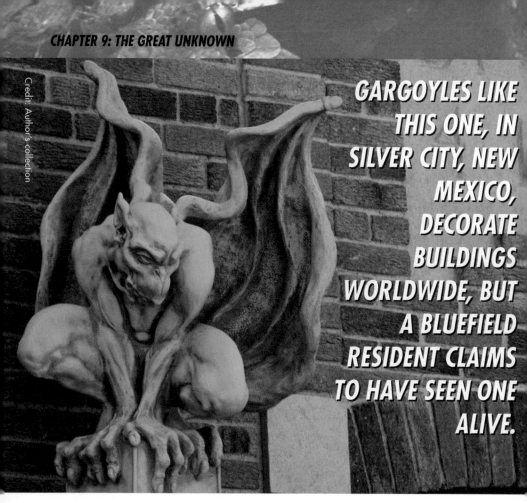

Credit: Author's collection

GARGOYLES LIKE THIS ONE, IN SILVER CITY, NEW MEXICO, DECORATE BUILDINGS WORLDWIDE, BUT A BLUEFIELD RESIDENT CLAIMS TO HAVE SEEN ONE ALIVE.

as if someone took the pause button off of me, I fled so fast to my home that I don't even remember the race getting there.[43]

Arriving home, Robert blurted out the story to his mother. She tried to calm him, paging through a Childcraft book of animals, seeking an illustration that would match the creature he had seen. "The closest animal that I could find that looked like what I saw was a koala bear," he later wrote, "but I only picked that animal out because it had similar black pointed eyes."[44] His mother reassured him that koalas lived far off, in Australia, suggesting that what he'd seen was a dog. Still haunted by the sighting decades later, he turned to the Internet, searching in vain for similar stories.

■

>> BLOOD TRAILS

WITNESS SAMANTHA PEYTON shared her story from Charleston on July 30, 2004, describing events from the previous night. During a sleepover with friend Terrianna, barking dogs roused the girls. They went outside with a flashlight, saw nothing at first, then "heard things that I have never heard before." The flashlight's beam fell on a trail of blood, which they followed to find a neighbor's freshly killed cat. Worse yet:

Something was eating it. Yeah, it sounds nasty but I couldn't help [watching]. Whatever was eating it had long pointy teeth and a long spiked tail with red fiery eyes. I couldn't think to yell, but it looked at my friend and me and growled. We ran and

it was coming after us. I didn't know what to do, so we ran inside.[45]

The creature stopped short of Samantha's porch, apparently intimidated by the outdoor lights. Samantha wrote, "We said tomorrow if this happens again we need to take a camera with us to see if we can get a picture of it. If we do it will be on this site [West Virginia Ghosts]."[46] At ten years and counting, that photo has yet to appear. ■

> AYEW? GESUNDHEIT!

TEN WEEKS AFTER Peyton posted her story online, witness Sarah Willis shared another, told by her grandfather "Doc" Carpenter. No date is offered for the incident, occurring on a hunting trip near Erbacon (Webster County). On the afternoon in question, seeking prey, Carpenter found that "he was being stalked by a creature that resembled a black panther with an almost 'bulldog' like face and red eyes." He eluded the creature, which howled after him, making a sound Carpenter rendered as "A-yeeew." Peyton's father suggested that it may have been "a panther that had been shot in the face," but I include it here, among the other great unknowns, for the uniqueness of its physical description.[47] ■

> 'ROO ON THE RUN

ON NEW YEAR'S DAY 2005, the DNR's office in Charleston received a call reporting a kangaroo at large in the city's suburbs. A dispatcher suspected the caller of being intoxicated, but reports rapidly multiplied. By June, a local TV station would declare, "The small male kangaroo comes out mostly at night or in the early morning, officials said. He makes appearances in backyards and on the county's rural roads."[48]

Misplaced kangaroos have been appearing nationwide for decades, some of them behaving in the most peculiar ways, but conservation officer Clyde Armstead had a theory about the Charleston marsupial's origin, suspecting that it escaped from an exotic animal farm in nearby Evans. "I spoke to someone who doesn't want to claim it," he said. "So I don't know if it has a name. But he does admit to having other kangaroos." Tracy and Dortha Pursley, owners of the farm, declined to comment.[49]

In early June, two sheriff's deputies and a state trooper tried to catch the 'roo on State Route 62, but it eluded them, leaving only a bystander's photo to verify its existence. By then, observers were divided as to whether it might be a wallaby—a smaller relative of kangaroos and fellow member of the family Macropodidae, native to Australia, New Guinea, and some nearby islands.

The hopping fugitive was still at large on July 15th, when Officer Armstead wrote online:

The Jackson County 'Roo is still on the lam. It has been visiting the local vegetable gardens and where ever it can find a source for salt. It is a private pet as far as I know, and not a part of any zoo. Most of the locals are getting used to seeing it hop around down here for now. I just hope it doesn't get hit by a car on the roadway or shot by a poacher before we can catch it.[50]

As this book went to press, no further bulletins had been released concerning death, capture or sightings of the Charleston kangaroo. For all we know, it may have slipped back into limbo like its many predecessors seen at large in half a dozen far-flung states since 1934. ∎

Credit: US Fish & Wildlife Service

A PHANTOM KANGAROO APPEARED IN CHARLESTON DURING JUNE 2005.

"PRETTY UNIQUE"

JULY 2010 BROUGHT AN unidentified nocturnal screamer to Goldtown (Jackson County). Resident James Harrison caught the eerie sounds on tape, but could not identify their maker. "It doesn't sound like anything I've ever heard," he told reporters. "I called the sheriff's department and the secretary told me she thought it was a ghost, but no one knows. It's one of those deals where one opinion gives into another one."[51]

Those opinions ranged from wolves and coyotes to "the second coming of the Mothman," but the howling beast remained unseen. Mark Harrison declared, "This is pretty unique. We've heard coyotes and turkeys and foxes and all that type of thing, but this is something we've never heard before." DNR spokesmen suggested the culprit might be an owl or a loon, but the Harrisons and their neighbors remain unconvinced.[52] ∎

A BLAST FROM THE PAST

OUR FINAL STORY COMES FROM an anonymous blogger, writing online in July 2004 of events occurring when his/her mother was eleven or twelve years old. The location, like the date, is undisclosed; we know the state only because the tale appeared on Jonathan Moore's West Virginia Ghosts website.

On the night in question, the blogger's mother was sleeping in a room "notorious for being haunted," at her parents' house. Around 11:30 p.m. she noticed an unexplained light in the yard outside and approached the window with a flashlight. According to the story:

What she saw in the window was a tall, slender female-like creature. It had dark smooth skin and small eyes that appeared to be red in color. The eyes reflected the

light from the flashlight and gave off a fierce red glow. Mom just stood there for what seemed like several minutes almost mesmerized by the hideous creature that had been watching her. When she came to her senses, she yelled for my grandfather. When she yelled the creature glared at her and let out a hissing cry before running off up the hill into the thick woods behind the house.[53]

The brief account leaves important questions unanswered. Was the prowler in more or less humanoid form? If not, how did the witness determine its "female-like" sex? Have any similar encounters been reported?

The answers, alas, are lost like the creature itself, in darkness. ∎

ENDNOTES

INTRODUCTION

1. West Virginia, http://en.wikipedia. org/wiki/West_Virginia. Retrieved March 30, 2014.
2. West Virginia Forests, www. wvcommerce.org/resources/forestry/ default.aspx. Retrieved March 30, 2014.
3. US Cities: West Virginia, www. togetherweteach.com/TWTIC/ uscityinfo/48wv/wvpopr/48wvpr.htm. Retrieved March 30, 2014.
4. Michael Newton, *Encyclopedia of Cryptozoology* (Jefferson, NC: McFarland, 2005), p. 3.

CHAPTER 1

1. Jodi Burnsworth, "Gone and Back Again: Cougars in West Virginia," http://theintermountain.com/page/ blogs.detail/display/134/Gone-and-Back-Again--Cougars-in-West-Virginia.html. Retrieved March 31, 2014.
2. List of mammals of West Virginia, http://en.wikipedia.org/wiki/List_of_ mammals_of_West_Virginia. Retrieved March 31, 2014.
3. *Calhoun Chronicle*, Jan. 24, 1911.
4. Mountain Lion Sightings, West Virginia, Case #58, www.richwooders. com/appalachian/wildlife/sightings/ mountain_lion.htm. Retrieved April 4, 2014.
5. Burnsworth, "Gone and Back Again."

6. Chris Bolgiano, "Living with Cougars in the Appalachian Mountains," www. patc.us/resources/florafauna/cougar. html. Retrieved March 31, 2014.
7. Harold E. Parsons, "Definite Mountain Lion Tracks," *Wonderful West Virginia* 41 (January 1978): 6.
8. *The Daily Mail* (Hagerstown, MD), April 7, 1976.
9. *The Daily Mail* (Hagerstown, MD), April 14, 1976.
10. Field Evidence of Cougars in Eastern North America, www.easterncougar. org/pages/6thworkshop.htm. Retrieved March 31, 2014; Todd Lester, "Search for Cougars in the East," *North American BioFortean Review* 3 (October 2001): 15.
11. Cougar Quest—Virginia, www.btcent. com/CougarQuest.htm. Retrieved April 1, 2014.
12. Skip Johnson, "Mountain Lion 'Sightings,'" *Wonderful West Virginia* 41 (October 1977): 15.
13. Frank H. Tighe Jr., "Mountain Lions in the Cranberry Back Country?" *Wonderful West Virginia* 42 (May 1978): 3.
14. Mountain Lion Sightings, West Virginia, Case #12.
15. Field Evidence of Cougars in Eastern North America; Kristina Sandi, "The phantom of Appalachia," www.mnn. com/local-reports/west-virginia/ local-blog/the-phantom-of-appalachia. Retrieved April 1, 2014.

16. Lester, "Search for Cougars in the East," pp. 15-17.
17. Cougar Quest—Virginia.
18. Ibid.
19. Ibid.
20. Mountain Lion Sightings, West Virginia, Case #65.
21. Ibid., Case #12.
22. Chris Bolgiano and Jerry Roberts, eds., *The Eastern Cougar: Historic Accounts, Scientific Investigations, and New Evidence* (Mechanicsburg, PA: Stackpole Books, 2005), pp. 113-14.
23. Mountain Lion Sightings, West Virginia, Case #51.
24. Ibid., Case #44.
25. Ibid., Case #17.
26. Ibid., Case #30.
27. Ibid., Case #58.
28. Ibid., Case #105.
29. Ibid., Case #31.
30. Cougar Quest—Virginia.
31. Ibid.
32. Mountain Lion Sightings, West Virginia, Case #66.
33. Ibid., Case #51.
34. Ibid., Case #6.
35. John A. Lutz and Linda A. Lutz, "Century-Old Mystery Rises from the Shadows," *North American BioFortean Review* 3 (October 2001): 31, 45-6.
36. Mountain Lion Sightings, West Virginia, Case #10.
37. Ibid., Case #19.
38. Ibid., Case #45.
39. Cougar Quest—Virginia.
40. Sandi, "The phantom of Appalachia."
41. Cougar Quest—Virginia.
42. Mountain Lion Sightings, West Virginia, Case #86.
43. Ibid., Case #62.
44. Cougar Quest—Virginia.
45. Mountain Lion Sightings, West Virginia, Case #44.
46. Ibid., Case #11.
47. Ibid., Case #15.
48. Ibid., Case #59.
49. Ibid., Case #1.
50. Ibid., Case #2.
51. Ibid., Case #4.
52. Ibid., Case #42.
53. Ibid., Case #54.
54. Ibid., Case #44.
55. Ibid., Case #5.
56. Ibid., Case #25.
57. Ibid., Case #54.
58. Ibid., Case #62.
59. Ibid., Case #8.
60. David Emery, "Mountain Lion Killed in West Virginia (and Elsewhere)," http://urbanlegends.about.com/ library/bl_mountain_lion_wv.htm. Retrieved April 3, 2014.
61. Mountain Lion Sightings, West Virginia, Case #14.
62. Cougar Quest—Virginia.
63. Mountain Lion Sightings, West Virginia, Case #91.
64. Ibid., Case #24.
65. Ibid., Case #20.
66. Ibid., Case #21.
67. Ibid., Case #22.
68. Ibid., Case #51
69. Ibid., Case #23.
70. Ibid., Case #26.
71. Cougar Quest—Virginia.
72. Mountain Lion Sightings, West Virginia, Case #33.
73. Panther/Mountain Lion Video in West Virginia, www.youtube.com/ watch?v=ao62AiFiZ-o. Retrieved April 3, 2014.
74. Mountain Lion Sightings, West Virginia, Case #34.
75. Cougar Quest—Virginia.
76. Mountain Lion Sightings, West Virginia, Case #71.

77. Ibid.; Kimberly Short-Wolfe, "Lions and tigers and bears...Oh my!" *The Inter-Mountain*, Aug. 15, 2009; Kimberly Short-Wolfe, "The continuing saga of Lily," *The Inter-Mountain*, Sept. 5, 2009; Kimberly Short-Wolfe, "Give us disclaimers and disclosures," *The Inter-Mountain*, Oct. 10, 2009.

78. Cougar Quest—Virginia.

79. Mountain Lion Sightings, West Virginia, Case #44.

80. Ibid., Case #46.

81. Tammy Marie Rose, "Mountain Lion sightings near Clendenin, West Virginia," www.examiner.com/article/mountain-lion-sightings-near-clendenin-west-virginia. Retrieved April 7, 2014.

82. Mountain Lion Sightings, West Virginia, Case #55.

83. Ibid., Case #57.

84. Ibid., Case #103.

85. Ibid., Case #64.

86. Ibid., Case #67.

87. Ibid., Case #68.

88. Ibid., Case #69.

89. Ibid., Case #70.

90. US Fish and Wildlife Service concludes eastern cougar extinct, www.fws.gov/northeast/ecougar/newsreleasefinal.html. Retrieved April 7, 2014.

91. Cougar Quest—Virginia.

92. Mountain Lion Sightings, West Virginia, Case #72.

93. Ibid., Case #76.

94. Ibid., Case #77.

95. Ibid., Case #82.

96. Ibid., Case #79.

97. Ibid., Case #81.

98. Ibid., Case #87.

99. Ibid., Case #88.

100. Ibid., Case #89.

101. Ibid., Case #94.

102. Ibid., Case #95.

103. Ibid., Case #97.

104. Ibid., Case #98.

105. Ibid., Case #99.

106. Ibid., Case #102.

107. Ibid., Case #104.

108. Ibid., Case #106.

109. Ibid., Case #111.

110. Ibid., Case #113.

111. Ibid., Case #114.

112. Rose Lee, "Berkeley Co. Residents Report Mountain Lion Sightings," www.your4state.com/story/berkeley-co-residents-report-mountain-lion-sightin/d/story/RIVk8V7EqUa6hx1yXvSXXQ. Retrieved April 8, 2014.

113. Edward Marshall, "Purported mountain lion sighting causes stir," *The Journal* (Martinsburg, WV), Oct. 16, 2013.

114. Mountain Lion Sightings, West Virginia, Case #63.

115. Ibid., Case #75.

116. Ibid., Case #3.

117. Chad Arment, *Varmints: Mystery Carnivores of North America* (Landisville, PA: Coachwhip Publications, 2010), pp. 628-9.

118. Ibid., pp. 629-30.

119. Ibid., pp. 630-1.

120. Loren Coleman, *Mysterious America* (New York: Paraview Press, 2001), p. 295.

121. Mountain Lion Sightings, West Virginia, Case #12.

122. Ibid., Case #52.

123. Ibid., Case #60.

124. Ibid., Case #110.

125. Black Panther?, www.wvghosts.com/archives/1365. Retrieved April 9, 2014.

126. Mountain Lion Sightings, West Virginia, Case #45.

127. Coleman, *Mysterious America,* p. 115.

128. Mountain Lion Sightings, West Virginia, Case #7.

129. Ibid., Case #9.

130. The Greenbrier County Monster, www.wvghosts.com/archives/1385. Retrieved April 9, 2014.

131. John A. Lutz and Linda A. Lutz, "Century-Old Mystery Rises from the Shadows," *North American BioFortean Review* 3 (October 2001): 31, 45.

132. Gulf Coast Bigfoot Research Organization (hereafter GCBRO), www.gcbro.com/WVpoca0002.html. Retrieved April 10, 2014.

133. Another Black Panther, www.wvghosts.com/archives/1358. Retrieved April 10, 2014.

134. *MonsterQuest,* "Lions in the Backyard," first aired on December 12, 2007.

135. GCBRO, www.gcbro.com/WS0072.html. Retrieved April 10, 2014.

136. BFRO Report #26279.

137. Mountain Lion Sightings, West Virginia, Case #49.

138. Ibid., Case #18.

139. Ibid., Case #108.

140. Ibid., Case #29.

141. Ibid., Case #30.

142. Ibid., Case #32.

143. Ibid., Case #35.

144. Ibid., Case #37.

145. Ibid., Case #38.

146. Ibid., Case #43.

147. Ibid., Case #60.

148. GCBRO, www.gcbro.com/WS0073.html. Retrieved April 10, 2014.

149. Mountain Lion Sightings, West Virginia, Case #100.

150. Cougar Quest—Virginia.

151. Panther Series: Kennison Mountain Panther?, www.traveling219.com/stories/marlinton-lewisburg/kennison-mountain-panther. Retrieved April 10, 2014.

152. Mountain Lion Sightings, West Virginia, Case #101.

153. Black Creature Watching Me, www.wvghosts.com/archives/1435. Retrieved April 10, 2014.

154. Mountain Lion Sightings, West Virginia, Case #109.

155. Coleman, *Mysterious America,* pp. 25-30, 292.

156. Henry W. Shoemaker, *The Panther and the Wolf* (Altoona, PA: Altoona Tribune Publishing Co., 1917), p. 14.

157. George B. Schaller, *The Serengeti Lion: A Study of Predator-Prey Relations* (Chicago: University of Chicago Press, 1972), p. 28.

158. Arment, *Varmints,* p. 631.

159. West Virginia Code § 20-2-51—Permit for keeping pets.

160. Coleman, *Mysterious America,* pp. 150-9.

161. Ibid., pp. 293-5.

162. Ibid., p. 142.

163. More Tigers in American Backyards than in the Wild, http://worldwildlife.org/stories/more-tigers-in-american-backyards-than-in-the-wild. Retrieved April 11, 2014.

164. Thomas, the Winged Cat of West Virginia, http://theresashauntedhistoryofthetri-state.blogspot.com/2013/01/thomas-winged-cat-of-west-virginia.html. Retrieved April 12, 2014.

165. John A. Keel, *The Complete Guide to Mysterious Beings* (New York: Main Street Books, 1994), p. 37.

166. Karl P.N. Shuker, *Dr Shuker's Casebook* (Bideford, UK: CFZ Press, 2008), pp. 13–29.

CHAPTER 2

1. Amphibians and Reptiles in West Virginia www.marshall.edu/herp/wvherps.htm. Retrieved April 12, 2014.
2. "Alligators relocate in area waters," *Washington Times,* May 24, 2005.
3. "Large Alligator Found in Waters of Lincoln County," WSAZ-TV Channel 3 (Huntington, WV), Oct. 12, 2010.
4. Kate White, "Alligator found along Teays Valley Road," *Charleston Gazette,* June 22, 2011.
5. Ibid.
6. "Alligator found in West Virginia sewer," WCSH-TV Channel 6 (Portland, ME), July 25, 2012.
7. Edward Marshall, "Martinsburg man finds alligator near home," *The Journal* (Martinsburg, WV), April 27, 2013.
8. Lee Moran, "Shoplifter steals baby alligator after hiding it under his shirt," *New York Daily News,* July 24, 2013.
9. "Caiman found in Mon River; reptile is killed by fishermen," *The Times West Virginian* (Fairmont, WV), Oct. 5, 2013.
10. Amphibians and Reptiles in West Virginia, www.marshall.edu/herp/wvherps.htm. Retrieved April 13, 2014.
11. Patrik Jonsson, "Hybrid man-eating pythons? Florida is on alert," *The Christian Science Monitor*, Sept. 15, 2009.
12. Eric Burger, "The very real threat of invasive, large snakes in Texas," *Houston Chronicle,* Oct. 13, 2009.
13. Chad Arment, *Boss Snakes: Stories and Sightings of Giant Snakes in America* (Landisville, PA: Coachwhip Publications, 2008), p. 343.
14. Ibid., p. 344.
15. Ibid.
16. Ibid., p. 345.
17. Ibid., pp. 382-4.

CHAPTER 3

1. Dwight Wickline, "Demon Rum," www.wvghosts.com/archives/1370. Retrieved April 15, 2014.
2. List of wolf attacks in North America, http://en.wikipedia.org/wiki/Wolf_attacks_in_North_America. Retrieved April 15, 2014.
3. Susan McNally, "Wicked, White, & Toothy—Mysterious Beasts of West Virginia," http://visitcryptoville.com/2013/06/10/wicked-white-toothy-mysterious-beasts-of-west-virginia. Retrieved April 17, 2014.
4. Jeff Ward and Allen Peyatt, "Demon Creature Spotted Again," www.wvghosts.com/archives/1369. Retrieved April 17, 2014.
5. Ibid.
6. Demon Creature, www.wvghosts.com/archives/1367. Retrieved April 17, 2014.
7. Ibid.
8. West Virginia Canid? www.beastofbrayroad.com/sightingslog2.html. Retrieved April 17, 2014.
9. Monster Encounter in Dolly Sods, www.phantomsandmonsters.com/2013/07/monster-encounter-in-dolly-sods.html. Retrieved April 17, 2014.
10. Ibid.
11. Beast in the Night!!!!, www.wvghosts.com/archives/1437. Retrieved April 17, 2014.
12. Pet Statistics, www.aspca.org/about-us/faq/pet-statistics. Retrieved April 17, 2014.

13. Chris Christoff, "Abandoned Dogs Roam Detroit in Packs as Humans Dwindle," www.bloomberg.com/news/2013-08-21/abandoned-dogs-roam-detroit-in-packs-as-humans-dwindle.html. Retrieved April 17, 2014.
14. Maryann Mott, "US Facing Feral-Dog Crisis," http://news.nationalgeographic.com/news/2003/08/0821_030821_straydogs.html. Retrieved, April 17, 2014.
15. "Fire Chief Shocked by Result of Wild Dog Attack," WSAZ-TV Channel 3 (Huntington, WV), May 31, 2011.
16. Mountain Men of W.V. Seek Mysterious Beasts of the Appalachian Wild in Destination America's New Series "Mountain Monsters," www.btvguide.net/Mountain-Monsters/Season-1/episode-3. Retrieved April 17, 2014.
17. The Devil Dog of Logan County WV, http://appalachianmonsters.blogspot.com/2013/11/i-have-been-watching-this-show-on-cable.html. Retrieved April 17, 2014.
18. Dog anatomy, http://en.wikipedia.org/wiki/Dog_anatomy. Retrieved April 17, 2014.
19. Robbie Shaw, "West Virginia Sighting," http://dogmanresearch.blogspot.com/2014/02/west-virginia-sighting.html. Retrieved, April 17, 2014.
20. Ibid.

CHAPTER 4

1. List of birds of West Virginia, http://en.wikipedia.org/wiki/List_of_birds_of_West_Virginia. Retrieved April 18, 2014.
2. "A Modern Roc," St. Louis (MO) Globe-Dispatch, Feb. 24, 1895.
3. Ibid.
4. Chad Arment, Cryptozoology: Science & Speculation (Landisville, PA: Coachwhip Publications, 2004), pp. 188-9.
5. "Gigantic Feathered Creature," Fort Wayne (IN) News, Feb. 1, 1896.
6. Steve Williams, " 'What' Done It?" Charleston (WV) Daily Mail, Aug. 21, 1978.
7. Ibid.
8. The Picnic, www.wvghosts.com/archives/1387. Retrieved April 19, 2014.
9. Stan Gordon, "Eyewitness Accounts: Was This A Close Encounter With A Thunderbird?" http://s8int.com/phile/eyewit33.html. Retrieved April 18, 2014.
10. Ibid.
11. Ibid.
12. Ibid.
13. Teratornithidae, http://en.wikipedia.org/wiki/Teratornithidae. Retrieved April 19, 2014.
14. Flatwoods monster, http://en.wikipedia.org/wiki/Flatwoods_monster. Retrieved April 19, 2014.
15. Ibid.
16. " 'Monster' held illusion created by meteor's gas," Charleston Gazette, Sept. 23, 1952.
17. Joe Nickell, "The Flatwoods UFO Monster," www.csicop.org/si/show/flatwoods_ufo_monster. Retrieved April 19, 2014.
18. Ivan T. Sanderson, Uninvited Visitors: A Biologist Looks at UFO's (New York: Cowles, 1967), p. 51.
19. Nickell, "The Flatwoods UFO Monster."
20. MonsterQuest, www.history.com/shows/monsterquest/episodes. Retrieved April 19, 2014.

21. James Gay Jones, *Appalachian Ghost Stories and Other Tales* (Parsons, WV: McClain Printing Co., 1975), pp. 93-6.

22. Ibid.

23. Mannix Porterfield, "West Virginia almost a UFO Heaven?" *Register-Herald,*

24. Keel, *The Complete Guide to Mysterious Beings.* pp. 246, 270.

25. "Eight People Say They Saw 'Creature,' " *Williamson (WV) Daily News,* Nov. 18, 1966.

26. Keel, p. 246.

27. Ibid., p. 247.

28. Ibid.

29. "Eight People Say They Saw 'Creature,' " *Williamson Daily News,* Nov. 18, 1966.

30. Ibid.

31. "Monster Bird With Red Eyes May Be Crane," *Gettysburg (PA) Times,* Dec. 1, 1966.

32. Keel, *The Complete Guide to Mysterious Beings.* pp. 269-73.

33. Jan Harold Brunvand, *The Baby Train & Other Lusty Urban Legends* (New York: W. W. Norton & Company, 1994), p. 98.

34. The Mothman Death List, www.lorencoleman.com/mothman_death_list.html. Retrieved April 20, 2014.

35. Joe Nickell, *The Mystery Chronicles: More Real-Life X-Files* (Lexington, KY: University Press of Kentucky, 2004), pp. 93-8.

36. Ibid., p. 98.

37. Mark A. Hall, *Thunderbirds: America's Living Legend of Giant Birds* (New York: Paraview Press, 2004), pp. 159-70.

38. Jerome Clark, *Extraordinary Encounters: An Encyclopedia of Extraterrestrials and Otherworldly Beings* (Santa Barbara, CA: ABC-CLIO, 2000), pp. 178-9.

39. " 'Mothman' still a frighteningly big draw for tourists," *Toronto Star,* Jan. 19, 2008.

40. Quoted by Jerome Clark in *Unnatural Phenomena: A Guide to the Bizarre Wonders of North America* (Santa Barbara, CA: ABC-CLIO, 2005), pp. 344-5.

41. Keel, *The Complete Guide to Mysterious Beings.* p. 242.

42. Ibid., pp. 265-6.

43. Lon Strickler, "Winged Manta Ray Shaped Cryptid Near Ashton, WV," www.phantomsandmonsters.com/2010/09/additional-ray-shaped-cryptid-sightings.html. Retrieved April 22, 2014.

44. Ibid.

45. Ibid.

46. Lon Strickler, "Additional Ray-Shaped Cryptid Sightings in WV Ohio River Valley Revealed," www.phantomsandmonsters.com/2010/09/additional-ray-shaped-cryptid-sightings.html. Retrieved April 22, 2014.

47. Ibid.

CHAPTER 5

1. Susan McNally, "Wicked, White, & Toothy—Mysterious Beasts of West Virginia," http://visitcryptoville.com/2013/06/10/wicked-white-toothy-mysterious-beasts-of-west-virginia. Retrieved April 24, 2014.

2. The Hello Thing, www.wvghosts.com/archives/1386. Retrieved April 24, 2014.

3. The Croup, www.wvghosts.com/archives/1384. Retrieved April 24, 2014.

4. Ibid.

5. White Thing of Ragland, www. wvghosts.com/archives/1438. Retrieved April 25, 2014.

6. Another White Beast Encounter, www.wvghosts.com/archives/1438. Retrieved April 25, 2014.

7. Sheepsquatch, http://carnivoraforum. com/topic/9685350/1. Retrieved April 25, 2014.

8. Ed Rollins, "Sheep-Squatch," www. wvghosts.com/archives/1377. Retrieved April 25, 2014.

9. Ibid.

10. Ibid.

11. Sheepsquatch, http://carnivoraforum. com/topic/9685350/1.

12. Another White Beast Encounter, www.wvghosts.com/archives/1438.

13. Sheepsquatch, http://cryptidz.wikia. com/wiki/Sheepsquatch. Retrieved April 25, 2014.

14. Strange Creature In Pt. Pleasant, www. wvghosts.com/archives/1380. Retrieved April 25, 2014.

15. White Thing, www.wvghosts.com/ archives/1400. Retrieved April 25, 2014.

16. The White Beast, www.wvghosts.com/ archives/1391. Retrieved April 25, 2014.

17. White Beast, www.wvghosts.com/ archives/1399. Retrieved April 25, 2014.

18. Another White Beast Encounter, www.wvghosts.com/archives/1438.

19. Ibid.

20. Hogzilla, http://en.wikipedia.org/wiki/ Hogzilla. Retrieved April 25, 2014.

21. Monster Pig, http://en.wikipedia.org/ wiki/Monster_Pig. Retrieved April 25, 2014.

22. M. C. McKenna and S. K. Bell, Bell, *Classification of Mammals Above the Species Level* (New York: Columbia University Press, 1997), p. 100.

23. The Terrifying Sheepsquatch, http:// cryptomundo.com/bigfoot-report/the-terrifying-sheepsquatch. Retrieved April 26, 2014.

CHAPTER 6

1. Lakes, www.wvencyclopedia.org/ articles/1285. Retrieved April 27, 2014.

2. Lake & Reservoir Search Results, www.lakelubbers.com/west-virginia-deepest-lakes-in-west-virginia-L59-C3/. Retrieved April 27, 2014.

3. Anonymous Lake Monsters of West Virginia, http://lakedragons. livingdinos.com/virginialakemonsters. html. Retrieved April 27, 2014.

4. Fish, www.wvencyclopedia.org/print/ Article/2181. Retrieved April 27, 2014.

5. WVU researcher discovers new fish species in Elk River, http://wvutoday. wvu.edu/n/2008/02/08/6507. Retrieved April 27, 2014.

6. Aquatic Invasive Species, www.wvdnr. gov/fishing/Invasive_Species.shtm. Retrieved April 27, 2014.

7. John McCoy, "Cross Lanes Youngster Catches Coal River Piranha," *Sunday Gazette-Mail* (Charleston, WV), Aug. 29, 2007.

8. Ibid.

9. Ibid.

10. Piranha fish caught in WV river, www. absoluteastronomy.com/ discussionpost/Piranha_fish_caught_ in_wv_river_96471246. Retrieved April 27, 2014.

11. Hoult River Monster of Northern WV, http://theresashauntedhistoryofthetri-state.blogspot.com/2011/02/hoult-river-monster-of-northern-wv.html. Retrieved April 27, 2014.

12. Ibid.

13. David Cain, "Ogua: The Rivesville River Monster," *Wonderful West Virginia* 63 (September 1999): 26-8.
14. Ibid.
15. Ibid.
16. Ibid.
17. Ibid.
18. Mike Dash, "Frank Searle's lost second book," http://blogs.forteana.org/node/95, Retrieved April 29, 2014.
19. Untitled article, *Pittsburgh Post*, July 8, 1893.
20. *Winnipeg Tribune*, Sept. 15, 1893.
21. Mark A. Hall, "Mysteries of West Virginia," *Wonders* 6 (2001): 123.
22. Ibid., pp. 123-4.
23. "2 Octopus-like Creatures Taken from State Stream," *Huntington Advertiser,* Jan. 11, 1946.
24. Ibid.
25. Hall, "Mysteries of West Virginia," p. 124.
26. Hu Maxwell, *The History of Randolph County, West Virginia, from its Earliest Settlement to the Present* (Morgantown, WV: Acme Publishing Company, 1898), p. 300.
27. Hall, "Mysteries of West Virginia," p.126.
28. William B. Price, *Tales and Lore of the Mountaineers* (Salem, WV: Quest Publishing Co., 1963), pp. 95-100.
29. Hall, "Mysteries of West Virginia," p.122.

CHAPTER 7

1. Henry R. Schoolcraft, "Observations respecting the Grave Creek Mound," Transactions of the American Ethnological Society 1 (1845): pp. 368-420.
2. Dave Cain, "Giants in our Midst? Tall Skeletons Reported Found in Marion County, WV," www.bibliotecapleyades.net/gigantes/MarionCounty.html. Retrieved April 30, 2014.
3. *The Western Literary Messenger* 27 (February 1857): 221.
4. Dr. Karl P. N. Shuker, *The Unexplained: An Illustrated Guide to the World's Natural and Paranormal Mysteries* (North Dighton, MA: Carlton Books, 1996), p. 151.
5. Cain, "Giants in our Midst?"
6. Samuel T. Wiley and A. W. Frederick, *History of Preston County (West Virginia)* (Kingwood, WV: Journal Printing House, 1882), pp. 8-9.
7. Cain, "Giants in our Midst?"
8. Ibid.
9. *Twelfth Annual Report of the Bureau of Ethnology to the Secretary of the Smithsonian Institution, 1890-'91* (Washington, DC: Government Printing Office, 1894), p. 9.
10. Ibid., pp. 418-20.
11. Ibid., pp. 425-27.
12. Ibid., p. 432.
13. Ibid., p. 437.
14. *American Anthropologist* Vol. A9 (February 1896: 66.
15. Footprints of the Ancients, www.pureinsight.org/node/1558. Retrieved May 1, 2014.
16. Glen J. Kuban, "The Texas Dinosaur/'Man Track' Controversy," www.talkorigins.org/faqs/paluxy.html. Retrieved May 1, 2014.
17. "Giant in Ancient Mound," *Washington Post*, June 23, 1908.
18. "Are Bones of Giants," *The Afro-American* (Baltimore, MD), Dec. 5, 1908.

19. Bob Teets, *West Virginia UFOs: Close Encounters in The Mountain State* (Terra Alta, WV: Headline Books, 1994), p. 96.
20. E. T. Badinski, "Men Over Ten Feet Tall," www.talkorigins.org/faqs/ce/3/part2.html. Retrieved May 1, 2014.
21. Nicole Lozare, " 'Dr. Dino,' wife guilty," *Pensacola News Journal*, Nov. 2, 2006.
22. Carl Wieland, Ken Ham and Jonathan Sarfati, "Maintaining Creationist Integrity: A response to Kent Hovind," http://creation.com/maintaining-creationist-integrity-response-to-kent-hovind. Retrieved May 1, 2014.
23. "Biblical theme park's finances investigated," *St. Petersburg Times*, April 18, 2004.
24. Ross Hamilton, "Holocaust of Giants: The Great Smithsonian Cover-up," www.xpeditionsmagazine.com/magazine/articles/giants/holocaust.html. Retrieved May 1, 2014.

CHAPTER 8

1. BFRO Geographic Database, www.bfro.net/gdb. Retrieved May 6, 2014.
2. Ibid.
3. BFRO Report #14739.
4. Chad Arment, *The Historical Bigfoot* (Landisville, PA: Coachwhip Publications, 2006), p. 330.
5. IBS Report #845, www.mid-americabigfoot.com/forums/viewtopic.php?f=167&t=5549. Retrieved May 6, 2014.
6. Gulf Coast Bigfoot Research Organization (GCBRO), www.gcbro.com/WVwayne0001.html. Retrieved May 6, 2014.
7. West Virginia Bigfoot Investigations Group (WVBIG), http://steventitchenell.tripod.com. Retrieved May 6, 2014.
8. GCBRO.
9. Ibid.
10. Keel, *The Complete Guide to Mysterious Beings*, p. 232.
11. Rick Berry, *Bigfoot on the East Coast* (Stuarts Draft, VA: The Author, 1993), p. 64.
12. Janet and Colin Bord, *Bigfoot Casebook Updated* (Enumclaw, WA: Pine Winds Press, 2006), p. 235.
13. Berry, *Bigfoot on the East Coast*, p. 64.
14. Keel, *The Complete Guide to Mysterious Beings*, p. 133.
15. Ibid.
16. BFRO Report #3582.
17. Keel, *The Complete Guide to Mysterious Beings*, pp. 133-4.
18. BFRO Report #38547.
19. Keel, *The Complete Guide to Mysterious Beings*, pp. 265-7.
20. IBS Report #3295.
21. BFRO Report #24421.
22. Ibid., Report #29124.
23. GCBRO.
24. WVBIG.
25. GCBRO.
26. BFRO Report #13949.
27. Ibid., Report #26963.
28. Ibid., Report #14037.
29. GCBRO.
30. BFRO Report #4237.
31. WVBIG.
32. GCBRO.
33. Ibid.
34. Berry, *Bigfoot on the East Coast*, p. 64.
35. BFRO Report #24945.
36. Ibid.
37. Ibid., Report #1201.
38. Ibid., Report #14037.
39. Ibid., Report #24061.
40. Ibid., Report #1207.
41. Ibid., Report #2786.
42. Ibid., Report #1200.
43. GCBRO.

44. BFRO Report #1207; Wayne Town—
Fort Gay, www.wvghosts.com/
archives/1015. Retrieved May 8, 2014.
45. WVBIG.
46. Ibid.
47. BFRO Report #14037.
48. Ibid., Report #23211.
49. Ibid., Report #7188.
50. Oregonbigfoot.com File #00932, www.
oregonbigfoot.com/report_detail.
php?id=00932. Retrieved May 8, 2014.
51. BFRO Report #1774.
52. WVBIG.
53. GCBRO.
54. BFRO Report #15475.
55. Ibid., Report #12959.
56. GCBRO.
57. Ibid.
58. BFRO Report #23191.
59. Ibid., Report #16228.
60. Ibid., Report #7474.
61. Ibid., Report #2786.
62. GCBRO.
63. Ibid.
64. Ibid.
65. BFRO Report #19206.
66. GCBRO.
67. BFRO Report #25062.
68. GCBRO.
69. Ibid.
70. New Report Received, http://
westvirginiabigfoot.blogspot.
com/2012/08/new-report-recieved.
html. Retrieved May 9, 2014.
71. BFRO Report #13122.
72. GCBRO.
73. Ibid.
74. BFRO Report #1206.
75. Ibid., Report #1204.
76. Ibid., Report #1205.
77. Ibid., Report #1203.
78. WVBIG.
79. BFRO Report #439.
80. Ibid., Report #1202.
81. Ibid., Report #3826.
82. Oregonbigfoot.com File #01010.
83. GCBRO.
84. BFRO Report #39812.
85. Ibid., Report #203.
86. GCBRO.
87. Ibid.
88. BFRO Report #7241.
89. Oregonbigfoot.com File #00924.
90. BFRO Report #2786.
91. Ibid., Report #12812.
92. Oregonbigfoot.com File #01507.
93. GCBRO.
94. BFRO Report # 8796.
95. Ibid., Report #3655.
96. GCBRO.
97. Ibid.
98. BFRO Report #26279.
99. GCBRO.
100. BFRO Report #15475.
101. BFRO Report #18793.
102. Ibid., Report #21894.
103. Ibid.
104. Oregonbigfoot.com File #00977.
105. Ibid., File #01507.
106. GCBRO.
107. BFRO Report #7727.
108. GCBRO.
109. Oregonbigfoot.com File #01003.
110. BFRO Report #11828.
111. Ibid., Report #14280.
112. Ibid., Report #14739.
113. Ibid., Report #23437.
114. Ibid., Report #10006.
115. Ibid., Report #10945.
116. Ibid., Reports #13083 and 11432.
117. Ibid., Report #13141.
118. Oregonbigfoot.com File #01761.
119. Ibid., File #01308.
120. BFRO Report #12862.
121. WVBIG.
122. BFRO Report #13237.

123. Loren Coleman, "What Is It? 'Braxton Beast' Photo Mystery," http://paranormal.about.com/gi/o.htm?zi=1/XJ&zTi=1&sdn=paranormal&cdn=newsissues&tm=124&f=21&su=p284.13.342.ip_p504.6.342.ip_&tt=2&bt=2&bts=2&zu=http%3A//www.cryptomundo.com/cryptozoo-news/what-is-it-new-photo-mystery-braxton-beast. Retrieved May 13, 2014.
124. BFRO Report #13312.
125. GCBRO.
126. Oregonbigfoot.com File #03744.
127. GCBRO.
128. BFRO Report #16529.
129. GCBRO.
130. WVBIG.
131. Oregonbigfoot.com File #03896.
132. BFRO Report #15250.
133. Ibid., Report #15355.
134. Ibid., Report #16890.
135. WVBIG.
136. BFRO Report #15481.
137. WVBIG.
138. BFRO Report #16204.
139. WVBIG.
140. BFRO Report #16204.
141. Ibid., Report #14739.
142. Ibid., Report #17449.
143. Ibid., Report #19841.
144. WVBIG.
145. BFRO Report #20846.
146. Ibid., Report #20068.
147. Ibid., Report #20101.
148. Ibid., Report #20159.
149. GCBRO.
150. BFRO Report #20863.
151. Ibid., Report #23411.
152. Ibid., Report #34043.
153. Ibid., Report #23648.
154. Ibid., Report #23762.
155. Ibid., Report #23411.
156. Ibid.
157. Ibid., Report #23648.
158. Ibid., Report #23477.
159. Rick Steelhammer, "In search of Bigfoot," *Charleston Gazette*, April 14, 2008.
160. GCBRO.
161. BFRO Report #24494.
162. Ibid., Report #14280.
163. WVBIG.
164. BFRO Report #28382.
165. Ibid., Report #25301.
166. Ibid., Report #25497; GCBRO.
167. GCBRO.
168. BFRO Report #25989.
169. Ibid., Report #26380.
170. Ibid., Report #26354.
171. GCBRO.
172. BFRO Report #27363.
173. GCBRO.
174. Ibid.
175. BFRO Report #30028.
176. WVBIG.
177. BFRO Report #31404.
178. GCBRO.
179. BFRO Report #27363.
180. GCBRO.
181. Beast of Bertha Hill, www.wvghosts.com/archives/1427. Retrieved May 18, 2014.
182. GCBRO.
183. Ibid.
184. Bigfoot Sighting In West Virginia, www.ghosttheory.com/2010/11/02/bigfoot-sighting-in-west-virginia. Retrieved May 18, 2014.
185. WVBIG.
186. BFRO Report #30154.
187. Ibid., Report #30028.
188. Ibid., Report #28702.
189. GCBRO.
190. Ibid.
191. West Virginia Bigfoot Vocalizations, http://cryptomundo.com/bigfoot-report/west-virginia-bigfoot-vocalizations. Retrieved May 19, 2014.

192. West Virginia Bigfoot Research Association, http://westvirginiabigfoot.blogspot.com. Retrieved May 19, 2014.
193. Thanksgiving Bigfoot Sighting in West Virginia, http://cryptomundo.com/bigfoot-report/bigfoot-wva. Retrieved May 19, 2014.
194. The Black Thing in Lewis County, https://www.wvghosts.com/archives/2246. Retrieved May 19, 2014.
195. BFRO Reports #35244, 37332, 36700, and 36662.
196. Ibid., Report #37565.
197. New Bigfoot Sighting in West Virginia, www.thecryptocrew.com/2013/01/new-bigfoot-sighitng-in-west-virginia.html. Retrieved May 19, 2014.
198. "Bigfoot spotting or high school hoax?" *Daily Mail* (London), Jan. 28, 2013.
199. WVBIG.
200. BFRO Report #41880.
201. WVBIG.
202. Harrison County, West Virginia, www.bigfootencounters.com/sbs/harrisoncounty.htm. Retrieved May 19, 2014.
203. McNally, "Wicked, White, & Toothy—Mysterious Beasts of West Virginia."
204. Oregonbigfoot.com File #00637.
205. GCBRO.
206. McNally, "Wicked, White, & Toothy."
207. GCBRO.
208. Ibid.
209. The Beast Of Boaz, https://www.wvghosts.com/archives/1382. Retrieved May 19, 2014.
210. The Red Eyes, www.wvghosts.com/archives/1389. Retrieved May 19, 2014.

CHAPTER 9

1. Thomas Jefferson, "Memoir on the Megalonyx," http://founders.archives.gov/documents/Jefferson/01-29-02-0232. Retrieved May 1, 2014.
2. *New York Times,* July 8, 1878,
3. Hall, "Mysteries of West Virginia," p. 120.
4. Ibid.
5. G. D. Douglas McNeill and Louise McNeill, The Last Forest: Tales of the Allegheny Woods (Dunmore, WV: Pocahontas Communications, 1940), p. 67.
6. The Mystery of Gauley Marsh, www.pocahontasoperahouse.org/event/mystery-of-gauley-marsh. Retrieved May 2, 2014.
7. *Columbus* (IN) *Daily Times*, Nov. 10, 1895.
8. 1890-1899 Humanoid Sighting Reports, Case No. 11, www.ufoinfo.com/humanoid/humanoid-1899.pdf. Retrieved May 2, 2014.
9. Ibid., Case No. 52.
10. Philip L. Rife, *It Didn't Start With Roswell: 50 Years of Amazing UFO Crashes, Close Encounters and Coverups* (Bloomington, IN: iUniverse, 2001), pp. 59, 194.
11. Quoted in Arment, *Varmints,* pp. 627-28.
12. " 'Blue Devil' Still Evades Traps, Webster Guns," *Charleston Daily Mail*, Dec. 8, 1939.
13. " 'Blue Devil' Mystery Grows As Strange Creature Kills Dog," Charleston *Daily Mail*, Dec. 13, 1939.
14. Ibid.
15. Ibid.
16. *Charleston Gazette,* Dec. 24, 1939.
17. "It's a Hard Life," *Charleston Gazette*, Jan. 30, 1940.
18. Ibid.

19. Hall, "Mysteries of West Virginia," p. 121.
20. Quoted ibid.
21. Ibid.
22. Kurt McCoy, "Researching the Grafton Monster!" https://groups.yahoo.com/neo/groups/grafton/conversations/topics/77. Retrieved May 2, 2014.
23. Keel, *The Complete Guide to Mysterious Beings*, p. 267.
24. Steve Williams, " 'What' Done It?" Charleston *Daily Mail,* Aug. 21, 1978.
25. Ibid.
26. Ibid.
27. Ibid.
28. Ibid.
29. Ibid.
30. Stalked By Wild Animal, www.wvghosts.com/archives/1378. Retrieved May 2, 2014.
31. Ibid.
32. Ibid.
33. Kyawiley Wildthing, www.wvghosts.com/archives/2241. Retrieved May 2, 2014.
34. Ibid.
35. Ibid.
36. Ibid.
37. Ibid.
38. The Creature Of Slip Hill, www.wvghosts.com/archives/1383. Retrieved May 2, 2014.
39. Weird Footprint Found In Creek Bed Near Milton, WV, https://www.wvghosts.com/archives/1393. Retrieved May 2, 2014.
40. Ibid.
41. A Scream Of Terror Of A Female Beast, www.wvghosts.com/archives/1357. Retrieved May 2, 2014.
42. Ibid.
43. The Gargoyle, http://paranormal.about.com/library/blstory_april04_29.htm. Retrieved May 3, 2014.
44. Ibid.
45. Strange Creature, www.wvghosts.com/archives/1379. Retrieved May 3, 2014.
46. Ibid.
47. Ayew Monster, www.wvghosts.com/archives/1364. Retrieved May 3, 2014.
48. Chandra Broadwater, "Jackson County has a roo loose," *Charleston Saturday Gazette & Mail*, June 17, 2005.
49. Ibid.
50. Ask the Conservation Officer, http://experts.wirefire.com/DNR/non-cgi/Forum1/HTML/004286.html. Retrieved May 3, 2014.
51. Matthew Earle, "Mysterious Creature May Lurk In Appalachian Mountains," WOWK-TV, Channel 13 (Charleston, WV), July 29, 2010.
52. Ibid.
53. The She-Devil, www.wvghosts.com/archives/1390. Retrieved May 3, 2014.

ABOUT THE AUTHOR

Michael Newton has published 279 books since 1977, with 10 more scheduled for release from various houses through 2015. Strange Monsters of West Virginia is his eighth Schiffer book, all but one of the others likewise devoted to cryptozoology. Unknown creatures have fascinated Newton from childhood, when famous Bigfoot sightings were reported from his home state of California. Early articles and books about the Loch Ness monster inspired him to visit the Scottish Highlands ten times over two decades, although he has yet to log a personal "Nessie" sighting.